Anxiety

INTRODUCTION

VARIETIES OF ANXIETY

AN IDEAL LIFE FOR THE ANXIOUS

HOW COULD WE BE ANYTHING BUT...?

How could we be anything but...?

It is, in a sense, astonishing that we ever manage to be anything but very concerned.

There is so much to which we are exposed, so many serious and unpredictable risks permanently waiting to threaten our peace of mind.

⏺▸ We live on a crowded planet, bathed in an atmosphere of dread, frenzy and ambition, and are forced to navigate around our vast technology-filled cities with a biological makeup better suited to a simpler, quieter, less excitable life in the savannah.

⏺▸ We dwell within painfully fragile physical envelopes, where something could give way at any time, a blood clot smaller than a full stop having the power to destroy us in an instant.

⏺▸ We are repeatedly compelled to make enormous life choices without the necessary facts and can have little clue what really awaits us around the corner.

⏺▸ Our long childhoods leave us open to every kind of turmoil and dislocation, our beautifully complicated minds being at risk of permanent trauma due to scars that we might have acquired before we could walk.

⏺▸ There is seldom sufficient time to connect with the quieter parts of ourselves or to grasp our uplifting unimportance in the grander scheme. We barely notice ourselves living. Our mass media continuously inflames our passions and fears while blinding us to the quiet, steady, undramatic kindness and hope all around us.

⏺▸ In relationships, we long to let down our guard but, at the same time, fear – not unreasonably – the grave hurt that may ensue whenever we surrender our emotions to another person.

●——➤   We put children on the earth and cannot be happy unless they thrive – and yet have no ability to protect them from fate.

●——➤   At work, our reputations could be destroyed in a moment by malice or error. We want desperately to win and yet are continually haunted by the spectre of defeat. We are never as young, beautiful or intelligent as we need to be.

●——➤   Our imaginations permanently remind us of everything that is missing, everything that might go wrong and everything that we might already have messed up.

From a clear-eyed perspective, the risks and troubles that face us are truly multitudinous and petrifying. Yet still people will sometimes casually tell us to 'relax' – as though such an injunction might be the work of a moment rather than the achievement of a lifetime.

Nevertheless, for all this, we should strive with deep seriousness to let go of one or two of our anxieties – by understanding them a little better, forming good habits to appease them and sharing them with a few kindly others – and thereby grow to enjoy the odd less worried day, when we can look up for a moment from our fretful thoughts and appreciate the wonder and blessing of being alive.

This is a book about anxiety and how to overcome it ✳

We're used to singing the praises of the human mind and body; they are, from many perspectives, truly astonishing pieces of engineering. We have brains capable of doing fractal equations, translating Finnish into Bengali and performing *La traviata* – and bodies that can scale the Matterhorn, send balls over a tennis net at 263km/h and create new life that can last up to a century. And yet, for all that, we should admit how questionably designed we truly are in many areas, if only to forgive ourselves for the mess and sadness we typically generate. It's not simply our fault that we're anxious; the machines we're trying to live through are riddled with flaws.

We are the outcome of evolutionary processes that have left us less than ideally adapted for what is required of us. Our anatomy is filled with redundant or vestigial organs. We have no need for our coccyx, the last part of our vertebrae that is the remnant of the tail that now gives us backache and growing pains. Nor do we have any use for our wisdom teeth, male nipples or appendices. And comparable vestigial problems exist in the mind:

Our wiring is massively and awkwardly oversensitive to our childhoods. Most of us still haven't dealt with our early years by the time we reach old age.

We tend to be unhelpfully mean towards ourselves. We're far kinder to most of our enemies – largely because we internalise methods of self-judgement that are modelled on some of the sternest judges from our personal histories.

We're very bad at thinking: we panic easily, we resist important thoughts, we long for distraction and are squeamish interpreters of ourselves. We have a devilishly hard time working out what job we might do, how we might tap our talents and what is truly driving us.

We get wildly over-concerned about some threats while ignoring others, especially the threat of not appreciating what we have while there is still time.

We can't correctly separate the real dangers from the false alarms.

We worry far too much about the consequences of others' views of us; we behave as if we still dwell in small tribes, where every piece of gossip could matter, and waste years improving our image in the minds of strangers we will never meet.

We exaggerate our chances of happiness – and suffer from bitter disappointment as a result. We can't gracefully accept just how likely it is that we won't be rich or won't have happy marriages – and rail at the unfairness of our condition, which is, in fact, just the statistical norm.

We have addictive tendencies, especially for food, alcohol, pornography and sitting on sofas.

We think of sex far too often, given the opportunities and our competing priorities.

And finally, of course, we are entirely biased towards being unhappy. Very little in our biology is interested in us being content. There must have been an early evolutionary advantage in being fretful and easily triggered: the others got eaten. Nature, apparently, would prefer we were worried ninety-nine percent of the time rather than lived in a relaxed way and fell prey to a tiger. So, we let the finest days pass without appreciation. We can't – naturally – ever 'live in the moment', a dauntingly ambitious and inadvertently cruel phrase.

In order to deal with our troublesome, ill-adapted bodies, we invented medicine, nutrition and exercise. To help us cope with our equally wonky minds, we need to lean just as heavily (as we do here) on philosophy, psychotherapy and self-reflection ✳

We've built a much safer and more prosperous world than our ancestors ever enjoyed, but modern times have also brought a special range of troubles into our lives that contribute to our enhanced anxiety.

Perfectionism

The modern age is ambitious. We wish to cure disease, waste no time, achieve constant happiness and live forever. These are fine hopes, but because they are necessarily still out of reach, they leave us angst-ridden, dispirited, disappointed with ourselves and angry with our societies. For most of history, people suffered greatly, but they were spared one particular agony: the sense that a perfect life could somehow be possible.

Individualism

For most of history, we lived in close-knit groups. The modern world has removed our reliance on the clan or the family and moved us to big cities where we can live privately and prosper on our own. We exist in an age of individualism. This may have liberated us in many ways, but it has also left us free to suffer alone and endure life without an anchor, feeling overly responsible for whatever befalls us and with no one to blame for our sorrows but ourselves.

The modern world is fixated on work. No social encounter can pass without the question of what we 'do' being raised – and only with a sufficiently impressive or elevated answer do we count as a valid and interesting person. Our self-esteem hangs upon our performance in an uncertain and random economy. Being nice is not enough. It is not surprising that the first great sociologist to investigate suicide – Émile Durkheim – discovered that the more focused on work a society becomes, the more its rate of suicide rises. It is not poverty or illness as such that drive us to the ultimate act of despair – it is the sense that we don't mean anything outside of what we've been able to achieve.

Modern societies firmly believe in the concept of meritocracy; that is, the faith that we should be free to make a success of our lives if we have sufficient talent and energy and that there should be no obstacles to our efforts based on class, gender or race.

However, this very well-meaning idea carries with it some alarming implications, for if we are to believe that those at the top truly deserve their success, then those at the bottom must truly deserve their failure. Under the aegis of a meritocratic worldview, an element of justice enters into the distribution of penalties as well as rewards. We move from thinking of the poor as 'unfortunates', deserving of compassion and kindness, to thinking of them as something far harsher: 'losers'.

A society that thinks of itself as meritocratic converts poverty from a condition of honourable, if painful, bad luck into evidence of personal incompetence. The burden of failure rises exponentially.

———————————————▶

The media

We're surrounded by a mass media that is hysterical, disaster-focused and vengeful in tone. It permanently gives us a sense that the outside world is extremely dangerous, that other people are mad or violent, that everyone is mean and that our societies are spiralling towards anarchy and degeneracy. Furthermore, the media holds up for ridicule and condemnation people who have made mistakes and thereby contributes to a feeling that no one ever deserves forgiveness or understanding.

Nature

Nature used to play an incidental role in keeping us calm. We were never far from the perspective-giving sight of a giant vista or an unspoilt landscape. Our attention would, in the past, frequently have been drawn to non-human elements, stopping us thinking of what happened to us as the measure of all things. Nowadays, we have no such relief. We live in concrete cages surrounded by millions of our own species; we have identified humans as the most important things that exist. It's a move that can be cast as a liberation, but it has unleashed claustrophobia and panic. There are now few established points of reference beyond us. What happens to us here and now in the city is framed as overwhelmingly important; it is all there is. And so everything that goes wrong, everything that frustrates or disappoints us, fills the horizon. The idea of something bigger, older, mightier, wiser and less known to which we owe love and attention has been stripped of its power to console us. We are seldom without our phones ✳

BASIC TRUST

*The greatest psychological achievement we might try and aim for
in relation to anxiety is what has been termed 'Basic Trust'.*

Basic Trust means that even though we can never know for certain what will happen, though we have no absolute guarantees as to how things will turn out, though we cannot wholly control our destinies and though there are some very uncomfortable dangers lurking in certain places, we maintain a belief that things are going to be – more or less – OK. They might not be so every day – there will be rocky moments... sadness or despair – but, broadly speaking, we have a gut sense that we'll pull through.

Importantly, this cannot ever be a firm knowledge; it is – in the true sense – a faith, a resilient belief in our survival and endurance outside of definitive evidence.

This Basic Trust might not sound like much but it is, in fact, the secret to a bearable existence.

This faith is, for most of us, a gift rather than any form of personal achievement, a gift bestowed on us by a childhood spent in the company of someone who felt (long before we were capable of it) Basic Trust in turn. When a drink was spilt, they didn't panic; they fetched a cloth and mopped it up. When there was a knock at the door at an unexpected moment, they didn't jump in surprise. When there was a reversal at work, they took it in their stride. When we felt angry and confused, they saw the bigger picture, interpreted us with benevolence and took us in their arms. And from these examples, we derived a sense that we dwelt among people on whom we could depend.

But many of us did not receive such a childhood. That is (probably) why we are here.

Yet importantly, the wisdom we didn't see acted out as toddlers can, with a little luck, be picked up in adulthood. Through a lot of thought, patience and introspection, we may come to a point where we too build up a bit of faith in the solidity of our circumstances, where we can take a few risks with people and with ourselves, where we don't need to be terrified of every new encounter or every new day – and where we can accept that even though we can't anticipate the whole future, we will be able to cope with whatever it happens to deliver ✳

VARIETIES

OF

ANXIETY

Anxiety belongs in every life. But in some lives, we can fairly say that it has become so constant that it is unnecessarily punishing. What can explain persistent, high-level anxiety that goes far beyond ordinary worry?

We might venture that somewhere in the history of the constantly worried, the bit of our mental equipment designed to distinguish between modest and extreme danger has taken a hit. The very worried have – somewhere along the line – received such a fright that pretty much everything has now grown frightening. Every slightly daunting challenge becomes a harbinger of the end; there are no more gradations. The party where one knows no one, the speech to delegates, the tricky conversation at work...these put the whole of existence into question. Pretty much every day is a crisis.

Let's go in for a metaphor. Imagine that at a formative moment, when the very anxious would have been profoundly unprepared and without the resources to cope, they had an encounter with a bear. The bear was beyond terrifying. It raged, it stamped, it crushed. It threatened to destroy everything; it was incomprehensibly, mind-defyingly awful. As a result, the anxious person's inner alarm jammed into the 'on' position and has stayed stuck there ever since. There is no use casually telling this person that there aren't any bears around at the moment, that this isn't the season, that most bears are kind or that campers rarely encounter them; that's easy for you to say, you who were never woken up by a giant grizzly staring at you with incisors showing and giant paws held open for the kill.

The result of this bear encounter is an unconscious commitment to catastrophic generalisation; the very anxious fear all bears, but also all dogs, rabbits, mice and squirrels, and all campsites and all sunny days, and even associated things, like trees rustling in the wind, or prairie grass, or the smell of coffee that was being made shortly before the bear showed up. The very anxious can't do logical distinctions: They can't rank threats accurately.

To start to dig ourselves out of the quicksand of worry, we – the very, very anxious – need to do something that is likely to feel artificial and probably rather patronising too. We need to learn – on occasion – to distrust our senses completely. These senses, which are mostly terrific guides to life, have to be seen for what they also are: profoundly unreliable instruments, capable of throwing out faulty readings and destroying our lives. We need to erect a firm distinction between feelings and reality: to grasp that an impression is not a prognosis, and a fear is not a fact.

One side of the mind has to treat the other with a robust, kindly scepticism: 'I know you're sure there is a bear out there (at that party, in that newspaper article, in that office meeting). But is there one really? Really really?' Emotion will be screaming 'yes!' as if one's life depends on it. But we've been here before and we need, with infinite forbearance, to let the screaming go on a little – and ignore it entirely. The cure lies in watching the panic unfold and in refusing to get involved in its seeming certainties.

We need to be like a pilot of a sophisticated aircraft coming into land in deep fog on autopilot – their senses may tell them that a dreadful collision is imminent, but their reason knows that the sums have been done correctly and that a smooth landing is, despite the darkness and the awful vibrations, about to unfold.

To get better, which really means to stop dreading bears everywhere, we need to spend more time thinking about the specific bear that we once saw. The impulse is to focus always on the fear of the future. But we need instead to direct our minds back to the past – and revisit certain damaging scenes with compassion and in kindly company. A consequence of not knowing the details of what once scared us is a fear of everything into the endless future. What sort of bear was it; what did it do to us; how did we feel? We need to relocalise and repatriate the bear, to get to know it as a spectre that happened at one point in one place, so that it can stop haunting us everywhere for all time.

That we were once very scared is our historical tragedy; the challenge henceforth is to stop giving ourselves ever-new reasons to damage the rest of our lives with fear.

Another way to put it is that the very scared are traumatised. Psychological trauma can be defined as a negative event so overwhelming that one cannot properly understand, process or move on from it – but, and this is the devilish aspect to it, nor can we easily remember it or reflect upon its nature and its effects on us. It is lodged within but remains hidden from us, making its presence known only via symptoms and pains, altering our sense of reality without alerting us to its subterranean operations.

Predictably, a lot of psychological trauma happens in childhood. Children are especially vulnerable to being traumatised, because they are congenitally unable to understand themselves or the world very well – and have to rely to an uncommon degree on parents who are frequently less than mature, patient or balanced. A child may, for example, be traumatised by a parent who – through no particular fault of their own – becomes heavily depressed shortly after childbirth. Or a child may be traumatised through exposure to a parent's titanic rage or violence. Or, because the widest category of psychological trauma is also the most innocuous, a child may be traumatised by what psychologists term 'neglect', which might mean that, at a critical age (between birth and five years old, and especially in the first eighteen months), it was not properly cherished, soothed, comforted and, to use a large but valuable word, loved.

The leading symptom of trauma is fear. Traumatised people are, above anything else, scared. They are scared of getting close to others, of being abandoned, of being humiliated and disgraced, of falling ill, probably of sex, of travelling, of their bodies, of parties, of key bits of their mind and – in the broad sense – of the world. The legacy of having been traumatised is dread, an unnameable, forgotten, unconscious memory of terror and fear projected outwards into a future. As the psychoanalyst Donald Winnicott observed: 'The catastrophe one fears *will* happen has *already* happened.' That is why, in order to find out the gist of what might have occurred to us long ago, we should ask ourselves not so much about the past (we won't directly be able to remember), but about what we are afraid will happen to us going forward. Our apprehension holds the best clues as to our history.

Crucially, and surprisingly, it can take a very long time before traumatised people even realise they are such a thing. A leading consequence of trauma is to have no active memory of what was traumatic – and therefore no sense of how distorted one's picture of reality actually now is. Traumatised people don't go around thinking that they are unnaturally scared; they just think that everything is terrifying. They don't notice their appallingly low sense of self-worth; they just assume that others are likely to mock and dislike them. They don't realise how uncomfortable intimacy is; they merely report not being happy in this or that relationship. In other words, trauma colours our view of reality but, at the same time, prevents us from noticing the extent to which we are peering at life through a distorted lens.

Only with a lot of time, luck, self-reflection and perhaps the odd breakdown do traumatised people come to a position where they start to notice that the way they think of the world isn't necessarily the way it actually is. It is a vast step towards mental well-being to be able to be usefully suspicious of one's first impulses and to begin to observe how much fear and self-hatred one is bringing to situations that truly don't warrant them.

Processing trauma usually works best when we can hook up our own malfunctioning and distorted brain to another more clear-sighted one – and can test our readings of reality against those of a wise friend or therapist. We stand to recognise that – to our great surprise – we are not perhaps inherently disgusting; maybe not everyone hates us; perhaps everything isn't headed for disaster; maybe we are not in line for a horrific punishment. And, crucially, if we do suffer reversals, maybe we could find our way out of them, because we are (and this can come as a true revelation) now adults, not a nine-month-old infant who underwent something awful.

Overcoming trauma is the work of years – but the beginning of the end starts with a very small step: coming to realise that we might actually be traumatised and that the world may not be the dark, overwhelming and dread-filled place we had always assumed it had to be ✳

TRAUMA EXERCISE

The leading symptom of trauma is to be daily tortured by a feeling of imminent catastrophe. Something terrible seems about to happen to us:

> We're going to be abandoned.
> We're going to be shamed and humiliated.
> We're going to be publicly mocked.
> We're going to lose physical control over ourselves.
> We're going to be seen as a loser, weirdo or monster.

The fear of such imminent catastrophes leads to a state of hypervigilance, where we are permanently on the alert, permanently worried, permanently scared and permanently really very unhappy.

People may try to reassure us, but reassurance goes nowhere; the terror remains.

One way to break the deadlock is to try to go back to the catastrophe that has been forgotten and that is making us sick with worry. If the future is to get brighter, we will need to remember the catastrophe and locate it where it really belongs: safely, but also poignantly and tragically, in the past.

It is strange that we should have forgotten the catastrophe. But that's the point with trauma; it disappears from memory. It is too painful to be held in active consciousness, to be processed and verbalised – and it therefore gets pushed into the unnameable, unknown zones of the mind, where it creates ongoing havoc.

To start to master trauma, we can reverse engineer a picture of what must have happened long ago, in years that we can't now easily think about; we can take what we fear of the future and picture that a version of this terror has actually

23

already unfolded. The best clue as to the nature of our difficult past lies in our fears of the future.

Imagine filling in a simple table. Start with the left-hand column first.

What I fear will happen in the future	What happened in the past
I'm going to be abandoned.	
I'm going to be shamed and humiliated.	
I'm going to be publicly mocked.	
I'm going to lose physical control over myself.	
I'm going to be seen as a loser, weirdo or monster.	

The logic of the exercise dictates that we should, for every entry in the left-hand column, be able eventually to think of an entry in the right. Bringing this to the surface is liable to be immensely difficult. One can't do it on command. It requires time, very relaxed circumstances, perhaps music, a long train or plane journey, a chat with a friend or therapist, a night or two when one stays up very late with a pad and paper and no phone and just thinks while the rest of the world sleeps.

But, eventually, some memories are likely to resurface, along with a lot of sadness and (ideally) compassion for oneself. One isn't about to be revealed as a monster; one was – already – made to feel like a monster. One isn't about to be abandoned, one was already left...

This doesn't mean that there is never anything to be afraid of in the present. But we have to draw a distinction between abject terror and fear. There are things to fear in the here and now, but these aren't things to be terrified of – and for one central reason: because we are adults and it is the privilege of adults to have a basic freedom, agency and independence. We can take action, were bad things to occur to us, in a way that children who were traumatised never could. Life may yet get very tricky for us, but we never need be as terrified of it as we were when the original catastrophe occurred.

Most likely, nothing as bad as we have feared will ever occur, not because we are lucky but because we were very unlucky in the past – and it is this bad luck, rather than something in the real world, that is leading us to be so unjustly and so cruelly afraid of living today. With sufficient exploration of the past, the terror of what is ahead could – just – be relocated to the category of historic trauma where it truly belongs ✳

The temptation, when dealing with anxiety, is always and invariably to focus on the ostensible cause of our worry: the journey to the airport, the forthcoming speech, the letter one is waiting for, the presentation one has to hand in...

But if we proceed more psychologically, we might begin in a different place. With great kindness and no disrespect, we may step past the objective content of anxiety and look instead at something else: how the anxious person feels about themselves.

An unexpected cause of anxiety is self-hatred. People who have grown up not to like themselves very much at all have an above average risk of suffering from extremes of anxiety, for if one doesn't think one is worthy, it must – by a dastardly logic – follow that the world is permanently and imminently at high risk of punishing one in the way one suspects one deserves. It seems to fit that people may be laughing behind one's back, that one may soon be sacked or disgraced, that one is an appropriate target for bullying and rejection and that persecution and worse may be heading towards us. If things seem to be going well, this must just be the deceptively quiet period before others are about to realise their error and mete out some horrific punishment. For the self-hating, anxiety is a pre-emptive anticipation of the pain one unconsciously feels one is owed; very bad things must and should happen to very bad people.

Part of the problem, and one of the curious aspects of the way our minds work, is that it isn't always clear that one is even suffering from low self-esteem; hating oneself has just become second nature rather than an issue one has the will to rebel against or even so much as notice. To tease out the sorrow and start to feel it again (as a prelude to treating it), one might need to fire a few questions at oneself ✳

A SELF-ESTEEM QUESTIONNAIRE

1. Broadly speaking, I like myself as I am.

○ Agree strongly
○ Agree
○ Neither agree nor disagree
○ Disagree
○ Disagree strongly

2. People should be relatively grateful to have me in their lives.

○ Agree strongly
○ Agree
○ Neither agree nor disagree
○ Disagree
○ Disagree strongly

3. If I didn't know me, I'd think I was OK.

○ Agree strongly
○ Agree
○ Neither agree nor disagree
○ Disagree
○ Disagree strongly

4. Growing up, I was given the feeling that I properly deserved to exist.

○ Agree strongly
○ Agree
○ Neither agree nor disagree
○ Disagree
○ Disagree strongly

If one finds oneself at the disagreeing end of such questions, it may be that one is an agitated person not because one has more to worry about but because one likes oneself rather less than normal – and certainly less than one fairly should.

The cure isn't, therefore, to try to dispel anxiety with logic, it is to try to dispel it with love; it is to remind the anxious person (who may be ourselves) that we are not inherently wretched, that we have a right to exist, that past neglect wasn't deserved, that we should feel tenderly towards ourselves – and that we need, both metaphorically and probably practically too, a very long hug.

The logic of this analysis is truly counter-intuitive. It suggests that when panic next descends, one should not spend too long on the surface causes of the worry but instead try to address the self-hatred fuelling the agitation. Anxiety is not always anxiety; sometimes it is just a very well-disguised, entrenched and unfair habit of disliking who we are ✳

If we were totally sane, we would respond to the present only on its own terms; we would worry or give way to anxiety only as much as the circumstances before us actually dictated.

But, of course, most of us are not-quite-sane, as evidenced by the way that we respond with such disproportion to certain events in the here and now. We have occasional tendencies to get wildly more worried and anxious than we should if we were simply following the facts in front of us.

What causes us difficulty is that we are wired to feel and respond according to precedent rather than on the basis of a dispassionate evaluation of the present. In particular we follow emotional tracks laid down in the distant past – when many of us were victims of deeply unrepresentative and unusually painful experiences, from which we continue to make panicky, gloomy and unhelpful extrapolations. In other words, we are, to use the inelegant but useful contemporary term, easily (far too easily) 'triggered'. That is, situations in the present elicit from us with undue haste responses formed by, and frankly better suited to, a past whose details we have forgotten and whose distinctiveness we cannot now perceive.

A tricky but not objectively existentially troubling email will hence convince us at once that this is the end. An item in the news will plunge us immediately into devastating guilt or boundless fury. The prospect of a party we have to go to or a speech we need to give brings on unbudgeable, monumental terror.

The triggering happens so fast that there is no chance to observe the process and see the way in which we cede our powers of evaluation from present to past. Our minds are simply flooded with panic, we lose our bearings, the rational faculties shut down and we are lost, perhaps for days, in the caverns of the mind. Even worse, not only are we not thinking straight, we're not quite aware that we aren't doing so. We mistake our agitated assumptions for sober truths. We're too panicked to notice that we are in a panic; we insist on our own stability of mind. So, whereas we should logically take to bed and declare ourselves unfit to think or plan ahead, we continue to sit in the cockpit of our lives and try to steer a judicious course.

We get triggered because we don't have a direct link to objective reality. Each of us approaches the outer world through the prism of an inner world with a more or less tenuous connection to it. In this inner world of ours lies a repository of expectations formed through our unique histories: our internal working models, or our best guesses, of what the outer world will be like, how others will respond to us, what they will say if we complain and how things will turn out when there is a challenge.

Crucially, and this is what we of course miss when we have been triggered, the inner world isn't the outer world. It contains generalisations and extrapolations from a past that may be far harder, stranger and more dangerous than the present. Psychologists have a handy rule of thumb to alert us to the disproportionate side of our responses: if we experience anxiety or anger above a five out of ten, they tell us, our response is likely to be fuelled not by the issue before us, but by a past we're overlooking. In other words, we have to believe (contrary to our feelings) that the alarm isn't ringing for any good reason.

The best way to free ourselves from being so easily triggered is to refuse to believe in most of what overwhelmingly and rapidly frightens or angers us. We must learn to adopt a robust suspicion of our first impulses. It isn't that there is nothing scary or worrying in the outer world whatsoever, simply that our initial responses are liable to be without proportion or without calculation of adult strength, resilience, resourcefulness or options. We should learn – at points – to try not to think at all until we've had a chance to drain the panic from our minds – or else to seek out other minds not as afflicted as ours in order to check our assumptions against theirs. Does it seem to them that the world is coming to an end? Do they think the police really are about to knock on the door? We need to calibrate our thoughts against those of a more equitable temper.

Another way to approach our panic and anxiety is to remember that, despite

*A TRICKY BUT
NOT OBJECTIVELY
EXISTENTIALLY
TROUBLING EMAIL
WILL CONVINCE US
AT ONCE THAT
THIS IS THE END.*

appearances, we are not a single person or unified 'I'. We are made up of an assemblage or a blend of parts dating right back to our earliest days. In a way we can't easily track, different events will engage with different parts of us. Some of our most troubled moments are when a difficulty in the present isn't handled by an adult part, but by a part formed when we were six months or three years old. We end up so scared because the challenge of public speaking or of a seduction or a worry at work has, unbeknownst to the adult part of us, been left in the hands of a very scared toddler.

In the circumstances, it can help to ask ourselves at points not what 'we' are afraid of but what a 'part' of us is worried about – and to learn more carefully to differentiate the parts in question. What might we tell a part of us in order for it not to be so scared?

It is a milestone of maturity when we start to understand what triggers us and why – and take steps to mitigate the most self-harming of our responses. Whatever our past seems to tell us, perhaps there won't be a catastrophe, perhaps we're not about to be killed or humiliated unbearably. Perhaps we have adult capacities for survival. Too much of our past is inside us in a way we don't recognise or learn to make allowances for. We should dare to approach many of our triggers like a starting pistol or a fire alarm that we will from now on, for well-grounded reasons, refuse to listen to ✳

One of the most difficult features of anxiety is that it tends to be all-consuming. It squats in the middle of our minds and refuses to let anything else in or through. Though the anxiety causes us great pain, it denies any attempts to be questioned, analysed, probed or reconfigured. We are both terrified and unable to think beyond our terror. Our thoughts become low, relentless, repetitive, stymied things: returning again and again to the issue of whether the door is locked, the accounts were signed off or the social media account is not under attack. Anxiety dominates and excludes any other form of mental activity; all that will be in our minds is terror. Impregnable and bullying, anxiety in effect shuts down our central faculties.

But there is one nimble way to try to outwit anxiety – and that is with a question that recognises a fundamental feature of anxiety: that it is frequently a smokescreen for something else, something beyond what we consciously think is worrying us, that we're in fact concerned with or sad about.

One of the peculiar facets of our minds is that we may choose to feel anxious rather than to confront things that may be yet more painful or emotionally awkward in our lives. It can be easier to fret than to know ourselves properly.

We might feel anxious about whether we're going to get to the airport on time as an escape from the greater challenge of wondering whether this holiday is even worth it and whether our spouse still loves us. Or we might get intensely anxious about a financial issue in order to avoid a trickier acknowledgement of our confusion at the course of our emotional lives. Or we may develop a sexual anxiety as an alternative to thinking about our sense of self-worth and the childhood that destroyed it. Panic may be invited to shield us from more profound sources of self-aware agony.

And yet, of course, we are always better off getting to the root cause of our troubles, rather than filling our minds with diversionary panic – and in order to do so, we would be wise, at points, to ask ourselves a simple but possibly highly revealing question:

'If your mind wasn't currently filled with these particular anxious thoughts, what might you have to think about right now?'

This question, as simple in structure as it is acute in design, is liable to unlock a moment of original insight.

The answer might go like this:

> I might realise how sad and lonely I am.
> I might realise how angry I feel towards my partner.
> I might realise how abandoned I feel.

And that, of course, is precisely what we should be doing now: processing all the stuff that our anxiety was trying to keep at bay.

Certain anxieties can be taken at face value, for they do clearly relate to worrying things in the world. But there is another class, and a rather large one at that, that is there for no better purpose than to distract us from understanding important parts of ourselves. If we need to suffer, and often we will, the least we can do is to ensure that we are suffering for the right reasons. At points, we should trade our anxiety in for something far more important – a confrontation with the real ambivalence and complexity of our lives – and we should do so thanks to a naively simple question:

'If your mind wasn't currently filled with these particular anxious thoughts, what might you have to think about right now?' ✳

Reputation might be defined as the claim that one can make on the goodwill of strangers; it is what your name will mean to those who don't know you, who spend almost no time thinking of you. It's what you will get reduced to when you aren't illuminated by love. How your reputation is assessed depends on the extent to which you have fulfilled, or violated, the ideals and aspirations of your society. Most of us are properly known to, and liked by, five to ten people. When it comes to everyone else, reputation is what will decide what we have been worth.

Reputation can't buy us love, but it can provide us with those valuable proxies: respect, honour and politeness. Those who are kind to us may not mean it, but they are at least making an effort. Not all of us crave equally the warmth that comes with a good reputation. Those with a particularly strong need for applause tend to be those with a weak sense of their own acceptability. The cheer of the crowd is asked to compensate for an innate feeling of shame. We seek the validation of the world when we are, inside, unconvinced that we are quite deserving. The more we have been humiliated, especially when young, the more the goodwill of strangers will matter; and – conversely – the more we have tasted genuine affection, the less interesting reputation can be.

The problem is that reputation is gossamer thin; or like a soapy bubble or an unstable chemical compound, some metaphor to suggest the ease with which it can be torn or destroyed. It is so prone to disappear because it is based not on knowledge or experience of one's deep self but on the candy floss of hearsay and third-hand gossip. It's the unconscious supposition of people who haven't thought very deeply about who one is and have absolutely no wish to do so either; it's what people who don't care about us think about us. This is what makes reputation so delightful when it is going our way. Our nobility becomes part of the unthinking common sense of the community. But this is also what makes things so tricky when reputation falls apart. The only way in which our good name might be rescued in the minds of others is if they gave us some thought – which is precisely what they have never done before and won't now begin to either.

Reputation will rise and fall according to how closely we track or depart from the ideals of our society – and these tend to be pegged to financial success, sexual propriety, decorum, marriage, sobriety, the sanctity of family and the purity of children. The more of these ideals one flouts, the harsher will be the penalties.

Unfortunately, we are – all of us – error-prone animals or, to put it more bluntly, idiots. We should say sorry to the universe every day, given how we are. We're impulsive, greedy, lustful, vain and selfish. Which means that every year, a small but significant section of the population makes an apparently minor mistake that causes terrible damage to others and blows up their life along the way. Not for nothing does Western civilisation have at its heart the example of Greek tragedy,

UNFORTUNATELY, I

ERROR PRONE ANIMALS OR

IDIOTS. WE SHOULD SA

EVERY DAY, GIV

which tells us of averagely good people brought low by highly understandable, everyday kinds of folly, for which they pay an ultimate price.

The whole community hears in an instant and one is done for. The punishment may be financial or legal, but the ultimate damage is psychological; one becomes a pariah. In the minds of all those who don't think about us properly (which is almost everyone), one is now a monster or a numbskull. For life.

From now on; we will need to be looked at through the eyes of love before we re-emerge as in any way human, that is, deserving of even a little pity or understanding. Only through love can we be remembered to have once been a baby, who was innocent, who struggled and who later made mistakes from passing weakness rather than evil. Only through love are there any other sides of the story.

As a result, all those who are not our intimates become sources of sure-fire damning judgement. We know from the outset that they will hate or condemn us. It becomes impossible to go to a party. One probably has to move town. Suicidal thoughts become harder to push away. Ambitions have to change entirely. Everything that depends on the minds of people in general is now impossible. 'What people might think' disappears from the calculation; it's a foregone conclusion. They'll think – always – that one is a demon.

When those in disrepute rediscover close friends and family (and they almost always do), it isn't coincidental or a cheap excuse: it's because they can see, more clearly than ever, that these are the people, the only people, who know them properly and can

ARE – ALL OF US –

O PUT IT MORE BLUNTLY,

ORRY TO THE UNIVERSE

HOW WE ARE.

therefore examine them with any degree of subtlety, as one might a character in a novel. For everyone else, one has disappeared into a single word of insult.

In older, more religious societies, there was the possibility of apology before a divine being, a period of penance and then, eventually, forgiveness. But that is one of the handy mechanisms we unknowingly dismantled when we decided that God was a fiction. We have been left with only one tool, the legal system, which levies fines and prison sentences but isn't in the business of restoring reputation – and doesn't get involved in most of the errors that cause it to be lost in the first place. There is, quite literally, in most cases, no way to recover reputation. The sentence is life-long.

We suffer also because we live in such vast societies. Recovery of reputation might have been possible when we lived in tribes of a hundred or so. You could go around and explain things in person, tent by tent. No such chance when it's a case of having a few hundred million minds to change.

So begins that peculiar challenge, leading a life without a reputation, a feat as arduous, in a way, as hanging on to a cliff-face with bare hands in high wind.

A few moves suggest themselves. For a start, acceptance: of oneself, of the situation, of one's misdeeds and of the darkness. Then, the construction of a new kind of communal life, one built around astonishing sincerity and vulnerability. One says it like it is. There is no need for yet more shame. A whole new set of friends is called for – before whom one can be truly oneself, in a way one never could be before things fell apart. It helps immensely if these friends have themselves lost reputation. Ex-convicts might be an idea. And fallen business people and politicians. They will have a kindness to them open only to those who have suffered infinitely for their errors. There is only so much empathy and thoughtfulness that blameless people can ever show. Animals are good too; they rarely judge. The immense open spaces of nature offer valuable perspective, as do history books.

Then one should, above all, make friends with Stoic philosophy in general and the philosopher Boethius in particular. For some 400 years across the European Middle Ages, one philosophy book was prized above any other. Present in every educated person's library, it was titled in Latin *De Consolatione Philosophiae* or, as we know it

in English today, *The Consolation of Philosophy*. Editions appeared in all the main European languages: Chaucer translated it into English, as did St Thomas More and Queen Elizabeth I, and Dante made it a centrepiece of the intellectual scaffolding of his *Divine Comedy*. It is one of the finer things one could read at moments of panic.

The book was the work of the Italian statesman, scholar and academic Boethius, who penned it in a few months in appalling circumstances in a prison in Pavia in 523 A.D. Boethius was born into a highly successful and wealthy family in the years after the collapse of the Roman Empire in the West. From an early age he took an interest in the Classics and translated much of Plato's and Aristotle's works from Greek into Latin; it is thanks, in great measure, to his efforts that classical philosophy made its way into the Middle Ages and then to the modern world.

For many years, Boethius's life was seemingly blessed. He lived in a sumptuous villa in Rome and was married to a kind and beautiful woman called Rusticiana, with whom he had two handsome, clever and affectionate sons. Under a sense of obligation to his society, Boethius eventually entered politics and occupied a number of elevated administrative positions under the ruler of Italy, Theodoric, king of the Ostrogoths. Bertrand Russell wrote of him: 'He would have been remarkable in any age; in the age in which he lived, he is utterly amazing.'

But suddenly, in the spring of 523 A.D., Boethius's fortune ran out. There was a knock at the door and a gang of Theodoric's guards accused him (quite falsely) of having plotted against the increasingly paranoid and vengeful king. With scarcely time to say goodbye to his family, Boethius was carted off to prison.

Entirely innocent, but also aware of the danger he was in, Boethius fell into despair. In a tiny cell, he contemplated his rapid fall from grace, his love for his family and the unfairness of his destiny. What would eventually lift his spirits – and, at the same time, gift humanity one of its greatest works of prison literature of any time or place – was his decision to think his way philosophically out of his sorrows.

As *The Consolation of Philosophy* opens, Boethius describes his listless sadness and terror at his state: 'White hairs are scattered untimely on my head, and the skin hangs loosely from my worn-out limbs.' But in this downcast state, Boethius receives an unexpected visit: 'While I

Unknown French Miniaturist, *Fortune and Her Wheel*: Illustration from Vol.1 of Boccaccio's
De Casibus Virorum Illustrium (On the Fates of Famous Men) [detail], 1467

was pondering thus in silence, and using my pen to set down so tearful a complaint, there appeared standing over my head a woman's form, whose countenance was full of majesty, whose eyes shone as with fire and whose power of insight surpassed that of all men....'

His visitor is a metaphorical figure whom Boethius terms Lady Philosophy. Lady Philosophy is carrying a pile of classical books in one hand and a sceptre in the other – and she has come to visit Boethius in his cell in order to remind him of some of the fundamental truths of his favourite subject, largely as defined by the Stoic school of Greece and Rome. That she should have dropped in on him was, in a sense, no surprise. In the classical world, philosophy was not an abstract academic discipline; it was a set of tools specifically designed to help one live and die well, with particular relevance at the darkest moments.

Lady Philosophy begins by gently chiding Boethius for 'flaring up against' his fate. She reminds him, as Stoic philosophers had constantly stressed, that human beings are not in control of most of what happens to them. Our destiny is, in large measure, in the hands of a devilishly powerful seductive goddess whom the Romans knew as Fortuna, the Goddess of Fortune. This figure was a central deity in the Roman pantheon and was represented across the Roman world on coins and statues. She was typically depicted holding a cornucopia in one hand, overflowing with fruit and luxuries, and in the other a tiller, a marker of her capacity to direct people's fates. Depending on her mood, Fortune might either shower us with gifts or, with a blithe smile, steer us towards catastrophe.

To be a philosopher means to understand all that Fortune controls, to resist her blandishments, to know never to put complete faith in the things that are, ultimately, always in the hands of an immoral and reckless force – and to prepare for the day when we may have to surrender her gifts at a stroke. These gifts comprise most of what we would today think of as the fundamental ingredients of happiness: love, family, children, prosperity, reputation and career. But, for a Stoic philosopher, none of them should be things that the wise should ever really trust – for all of them can be lost in horrific circumstances at any moment.

Lady Philosophy sits with Boethius in his cell and reminds him of his appalling exposure to Fortune's deceptive charm: 'I know the many disguises of that monster, Fortune, and the extent to which she seduces with friendship the very people she is striving to cheat, until she overwhelms them with unbearable grief at the suddenness of her desertion.'

But Lady Philosophy also reminds Boethius that the wise have to resist putting their faith in the gifts of Fortune. She introduces a famous image of a Wheel of Fortune, which spins between success and favour – and appalling punishment and pain. Fortune spins the wheel with abandon and merciless cruelty, enjoying the screams of those who, only hours before, were confident of their future.

'If you are trying to stop her wheel from turning, you of all men are the most obtuse,' Lady Philosophy tells Boethius. 'You are seeking to regain what really did not belong to you.'

Fortune herself pipes up at this point and says with chilling candour: 'Inconstancy is my very essence; it is the game I never cease to play as I turn my wheel in its ever changing circle…. Yes, rise up on my wheel if you like, but don't count it an injury when by the same token you begin to fall, as the rules of the game will require…. Isn't this what tragedy commemorates with its tears and tumult?'

Lady Philosophy now gets to the heart of her message. Boethius must, like any good philosophically inclined person, stop trusting in anything that Fortune can take away at once: 'You know there is no constancy in human affairs, when a single swift hour can often bring a man to nothing. If you are in possession of yourself you will possess something you would never wish to lose and something Fortune could never take away…. Happiness cannot consist in things governed by chance.'

Boethius must retreat to what the Stoic philosophers called his 'inner citadel'; a minimal self immune from the cruelty of Fortune. Lady Philosophy stresses that a different sort of happiness can be found by focusing on all that Fortune can never make one lose, specifically one's powers of reasoning, which give one access to the beauty, mystery and complexity of the universe. True philosophers rise above their immediate circumstances, become indifferent to their own fate and identify with the vast forces of history and nature.

It's a measure of the relevance of Boethius's message that we today so firmly identify happiness with two areas that lie entirely in the hands of Fortune: romantic love and career success. And, unsurprisingly, we are continually let down here, too, the wheel of fortune spinning us randomly from promise to disgrace, from hope to ruin. Boethius's provocative message to his own times and to our own is that the best way to find peace of mind may be to perceive the ingredients we associate with happiness as, in truth, direct conduits to a fundamental instability, and thereby to inner torment and anxiety.

Boethius's wisdom was to be the last eloquent outcry of the guiding ideas of classical philosophy and, in particular, its Stoic branch. Thereafter, Christianity subsumed its insights, which were then further obscured by the scientific optimism of the modern period.

Our own troubled times deserve to witness the rediscovery of the Stoic message. We become philosophers not by writing books or attending university courses, but by appreciating how little of our lives is in our hands, the ubiquity and fickleness of Fortune and our need to look beyond public opinion, family, love and status in order to build up serenity through the exercise of one's distinctive and fate-independent mental powers.

Boethius was killed, as he feared, a few months after being imprisoned. His grave lies in the church of San Pietro in Ciel d'Oro in Pavia, half an hour from Milan. In his honour, we should leave space for Lady Philosophy occasionally to come and visit us – and, when we are facing the worst turns of Fortune's wheel, let her strengthen our resolve to depend a little less on what was, in fact, never really ours to rely upon ✳

We all require truly good friends; but those among us who suffer from high anxiety need them especially badly, for one of the principal solutions to anxiety is – as we shall see – the company of the right kind of others.

However, we tend too quickly to think we know what we mean by a 'good friend'. It is easy to confuse the genuine with the ersatz article. Both may show up for dinner, both may seem outwardly kind, both will claim to be loyal – but only one will live up to the true calling of the word 'friend' and so stand any chance of sincerely assisting the soul of the anxious.

Here is some of what makes a genuinely good friend.

1. They have suffered

It sounds odd to demand it but it is a fundamental prerequisite that good friends need to have suffered. Quite a lot. However convenient it would be if people could be born friendly and empathise spontaneously with the pains of others, the awkward truth is that the human mind is too sluggish and selfish an instrument properly to imagine what suffering might look like for someone else until it has been energetically goaded on by its own agonies. Empathy has to be forged by personal suffering. To be a good friend, one has no option other than to have had close-up, personal experience of terrible times. One needs to have known at least a few of the following: illness (physical and mental), humiliation, reversal, bullying, financial disaster, public shaming, childhood neglect, isolation, defeat and panic. One needs to have wept all night, raged at oneself and thought one's very existence an error. Happy people unmarked by life can be many things: a good friend is not one of them.

However, suffering on its own is not enough, for it may – at its worst – simply lead to indignant self-righteousness, whereby the sufferer is convinced that it was everyone else's fault, that they are pure and the world is bad; in other words, to being a prig. The truly kind friend, however, is someone who has been inducted to a more sombre, important and painful truth still: the knowledge that a lot of what went wrong *was* their fault. Part of their calamities came down to their idiocy, their narrow-mindedness, their foolishness. They aren't focused on hating anyone else, they've given up pride and blame. They've been a blunderhead and they know it. This is what makes the good friend so sympathetic to your errors and slips. They know from the inside how one can be a decent person and yet still unleash disaster. They don't believe in their own innocence and nor do they in any way demand yours: they just know from experience how much every one of us stands in need of forgiveness and they're ready to give it to you in spades.

One of the fastest ways to turn into a monster is to believe that the world might be fair. If it's fair, there's no need to think kindly or imaginatively about the tramp, the prisoner and the outcast. They entirely deserve their fate and damnation. Nor is there any need to be sceptical about what the papers say and who is being lauded as 'righteous' or 'noble'; the established value system is obviously correct – and need only be followed in its entirety. The mob have it right. But the moment one realises that the world is, in fact, hideously random and unfair, that judgements can be corrupt, that rewards don't neatly track goodness, then everything at once gets a lot more complicated – and a lot kinder too. Suddenly, the beggar and the outcast might deserve your sympathy and the self-righteous crowd might deserve your scepticism. Good people can end up in trouble. Sinners can be worthy of another chance. The true friend is ready to give unconditional love, because they know the absurdity and cruelty of many of the conditions currently placed on love.

Ambitious people are evidently a huge asset to humanity; they get things done, their self-importance powers history and the progress of society depends on their acute self-regard. When they meet with you for dinner, they're always subtly keen to let you know how things are advancing for them – and they keep the score, as though the whole of life were a gigantic school exam and there was a big tick waiting for the winners on the other side of death. What these people can't be, however, is a good friend, for what that means is surrendering on shining in the eyes of an imagined fancy audience. Good friends don't give a damn about 'what people think' anymore (even if they might have done when younger). They're out of the 'game' (probably pushed out of it by their own mistakes), and they don't go after claps or gongs. What they're interested in, in the time that remains, is sincere communion. They want to hang around with other broken honest people and, without airs and graces, exchange kindness and support. They care about you because – remarkably, in one of the greatest achievements any human is capable of – they've outgrown any shred of preening fascination with themselves.

To summarise, the good friend has been humbled, they've given up pride, they've messed up – and they've drawn all the right conclusions from their troubles: that the only thing that counts is kindness. That's why they're going to be so patient with you; that's why they'll understand all the things you worry about and that you regret; that's why they'll be on hand with compassion, gentleness and plenty of rich dark laughter. If one meets with just one or two such people in a lifetime, one will have been properly blessed and will be a whole lot calmer too ✳

COMMUNION

&

ANXIETY

Anxiety and dread thrive in conditions of loneliness. Not only is one wretched, one feels convinced that one is the only one to feel as such. One's suffering lacks legitimacy in one's own eyes. To the affliction of anxiety, the burden of shame is too often added.

That is why, when anxiety starts to descend, there is one solution that is more effective than any other, that functions faster than any pill, meditation technique or book: *talking to someone kind who knows anxiety from the inside.* One needs to get oneself – fast – into a group and unburden oneself among thoughtful and good-natured people who have been visited by comparable pain, and who can respond to your confessions with infinite understanding. It helps immeasurably to sit with folk who know what it's like to be terrified, not to dare to leave the house, to panic at work, to be triggered by 'small things' that others would find innocuous and to be bullied mercilessly by one's own mind.

Every anxious person would, ideally, equip themselves with a support group and turn to them once a week or more. We'd gather at someone's house, chat about how things had been going and swap stories of our challenges. We'd in turn recognise some of our most private moments in the stories of others and be granted a rare opportunity to reconceive of ourselves as fundamentally normal and human – though very much afflicted. Our sufferings do not make us unique – they provide an essential opportunity to loosen our fears and bind ourselves together around a commitment to mutual assistance and kindness ❄

Going to parties is meant to be an ordinary and unremarkable activity: for the anxious, it typically presents one of the greatest of all of life's challenges. The idea of being in a noisy room filled with unpredictable and sometimes unknown others sets off every alarm.

To begin to calm ourselves down, we deserve to take full stock of just how weird parties actually are when considered objectively. There is nothing normal at all about being expected to feel at ease when one can be observed by dozens of pairs of eyes; when at any moment a 'frenemy' may approach with unwelcome news; when one is expected to feel happy to hear of the good fortune of others; when we have to encounter a random selection of people who may make one feel inadequate and envious.... In evolutionary terms, our brains aren't well set up to deal with parties. We were made to deal with small groups we might have known since childhood. We are not odd at all for finding parties hugely bizarre and, for the most part, horrifying.

We should dare to push back against the assumption that it is therefore indispensable for us to attend parties. Perhaps we can, going forward, dare to define ourselves as people who just don't do parties, as others may resist swimming or heights.

We can also question whether this means we are in any way antisocial. Modern society pushes the notion that sociability naturally springs up when lots of people are put together in a room; that it means speaking a lot and being notably cheerful about things that have been happening in our lives; that it depends on a jokey manner and – ideally – on the possession of a few entertaining anecdotes, often involving striking coincidences. But such assumptions sidestep two sizeable objections. First, perhaps true sociability – that is, a real connection between two people – is almost never built up via anything cheerful. It is the result of making ourselves vulnerable before another person, by revealing something that is lost, confused, lonely and in pain within us. We build genuine connections when we dare to exchange thoughts that might leave us open to humiliation and judgement; we make real friends through sharing in an uncensored and frank way a little of the agony and confusion of being alive.

Secondly, true sociability requires honesty. At parties, we are generally under such pressure to appear normal, self-possessed and solid, we are understandably disinclined spontaneously to disclose our true selves. Our default mode is – without anything sinister being meant by this – to lie about who we are and what is really going on in our lives. This suggests that a genuinely social occasion might be rather different from what we typically envisage. We think of a 'good host' as someone who makes sure there is enough wine and, at a pinch, ensures people know each other's names. But, in the profound sense, a good host is someone who creates the conditions in which strangers can start to feel safe about being sad, anxious and desperate.

A commitment to deep sociability might lead us to recognise that we depend on a little artful choreography to get us into the psychological zone in which true connections can unfold. We might need encouragement – and even a helpful lanyard – to share a little of what is sad within us. We need help in networking, not in order to find new investment opportunities, but so as to identify shared regrets, humiliations and feelings of despair.

Parties as they are currently structured constitute a clever ruse by a sharp minority, perhaps only ten percent of humanity, to persuade the rest of us that we have been provided with the social contact we crave. But, in truth, it takes a sharply insular and misanthropic person to feel that what goes on in an average party really counts as anything like the requisite encounter with one's fellow human animal. If we have a lingering horror of parties, we should be generous towards our hunches. It doesn't mean that we don't like other people, rather that we have too ambitious a conception of social contact to put up with what is on offer at most parties. The mark of a truly sociable person might, in many situations, simply be a strong desire to stay at home ✳

During a panic attack, the pervasive worry that we normally carry within us, and that is typically content merely gently to corrode away our lives, promptly changes tack and decides it might try to kill us off instead – preferably very soon.

We're meant to give an hour-long speech in a couple of minutes but we stand petrified in the wings of the theatre, our mouth entirely dry, our heart racing and our mind unable to remember so much as the first letters of the alphabet, let alone what our name is.

The aeroplane doors close and we realise that we won't be able to get off for six hours, that we can hardly move our legs without touching passengers on every side, that the air we're breathing has passed through the lungs of 200 other people (and a couple of jet engines too) and that we're going to be a few miles off the ground – and the whole situation suddenly seems wholly surreal, tear-jerkingly cruel and deeply unsurvivable.

Or we're at a business meeting, surrounded by colleagues and prospective clients, and we're made aware that our bowels are about to open or our stomachs to heave their contents across the table and that we'll be publicly reduced to a pure emanation of noxious sludge – after which it would evidently be best not to try to continue with one's life and instead to be taken away, done in and never mentioned again.

What are we to do at such moments? What could the most well-wrought philosophy do for us when we're about to soil ourselves or start wailing uncontrollably at the back of a tightly packed aeroplane?

There might, in spite of everything, be a few shreds of advice to hold on to: First, we should embrace the situation. Though this seems like the oddest and most embarrassing thing ever to have unfolded, it happens all the time, even to good, decent people who are worthy of respect and will enjoy a lengthy and dignified old age. This is not the end, though – of course – it feels exactly like it.

Second, accept the fear; don't fight it. It's like trying to wrestle with the current – best to let the waves carry one this way and that; they'll tire eventually and set one back on shore. Never struggle against a rip tide. Accept that maybe the speech won't happen; you might faint in your seat or be forced to run out of the room. So what? Refuse to be humiliated by the panic. You don't have to be competent all the time. Everyone is allowed some failures, and this just happens to be one of your well-earned ones.

Third, when calm has returned, try to think all this through, ideally with a kindly friend or therapist. It's to do – perhaps in part – with a baseline sense of unworthiness. You don't, at some level, feel it's permissible for you to give a speech and impress a hundred people or succeed in your career. Maybe, in your unconscious, this might make someone (a parent?) feel jealous or inadequate – and it's kinder, therefore, to stick to being small and unobtrusive.

To which the answer is to reassert, in the light of day, the basic truth that you have every right to exist and draw pleasure from this life, that there is nothing illegal about having a positive effect on others, that you can be a decent colleague, friend, parent and citizen – and make it to the bathroom on time. You are allowed to be.

Also, consider that the panic might have to do with a memory of long ago having been appallingly controlled, hurt and not allowed to get away. It's an aeroplane door that has just closed but, in the unconscious mind, it's perhaps also symbolic of a return to other situations of powerlessness that were unmasterable and continue to haunt you.

To which the answer is to go back to the past, understand it fully and drain it of its power to upset the present. The memories need to be heard and the trauma digested. Meanwhile, the plane is going to take off and the doors will eventually open again and one will be free to go wherever one wants because one is now an adult, with all the agency and liberty that word should imply.

Or maybe what powers your terror is a feeling that you have to impress other people and won't be forgiven if you don't. To which the answer is that you're OK just as you are; the days of having to impress are over; you need to prove nothing at all. There is no need to let self-contempt keep tearing you apart.

Fourth, at the height of the fear, it can help to get deeply but redemptively pessimistic about everything. Though it seems like everything matters intensely, gloriously, in truth, nothing matters at all. Almost every human on the planet is entirely indifferent to you. Out in the Mojave Desert, scorpions are scuttling among the rocks; an eagle is soaring above the Karakoram Pass; up there in the universe, the two moons of Mars, Phobos and Deimos, are completing their orbits. You will soon enough be dead, properly inert rather than merely scared, and it will have been as if you never existed. You are but a blip in eternal cosmic time; whether your speech unfolds well or badly, or you soil your trousers or not, is a matter of sublime, beautiful indifference to planet Kepler-22b, 587 light-years from Earth in the constellation of Cygnus.

Lastly, don't avoid everything that scares you; don't let the panic reduce you. Don't accord the fear so much respect that you start to listen to its tyrannical dictates.

Answer the aggression within every panic attack with its opposite: a deeply unconditional love towards you, its unfortunate, blameless, worthy and loveable victim ❋

It is natural to assume, at the outset of adult life, that being well known to others will help one to feel grounded, liked and safe. One will be exchanging the coldness of anonymity for the embrace of the world; long years of indifference by parents, siblings or school mates can be compensated for by a wider, more enthusiastic fraternity. Wherever one shows up, people will start to know who one is, and be a little impressed, without one having to explain too much. One will be the recipient of the near-automatic kindness and goodwill of strangers; one will, finally, with luck, fit in.

It's with such hopes in mind that one can be drawn to set up a social media account and share carefully curated thoughts and images with a growing band of followers. Or seek to make a name for oneself in sport, business or the arts. Or run for public office or a company leadership role. And with talent and a good headwind, one may, however modestly, start to become a little 'known' (that is, asymmetrically known to people one doesn't know oneself).

It may feel rather nice for a little while – but, soon enough, one is liable to come face to face with one of the less-often acknowledged facets of being in the public eye: the envy, resentment and eventual hatred of others (a sufficient number of others to create genuine agony). Every increase in one's own visibility generates – by a kind of inevitable emotional calculus – a degree of humiliation for those still in relative obscurity and therefore a momentum in sections of the audience to attack one's character in order to return to the status quo. There is no public success that does not, simultaneously, lead certain people to experience new feelings of failure – and so to develop desires for vengeance and comeuppance. As one's star rises, so too other people (perhaps initially obscured and reticent), often in one's own field or cohort, will experience themselves as more

At some point, one will make an error. It might be very small and quite understandable, except that rather than being forgiven and understood (as one might be by friends), one will find oneself at the receiving end of an extraordinary outpouring of anger, sanctimony and moralism. The bullying will begin – and though it might at first appear accidental and passing, one will discover an iron-clad law of publicity: that one cannot ever be reliably loved and steadily approved of by large numbers of strangers without being assailed by the resentment of others. The newspaper clippings and social media accounts will attest to as much, containing as they will constant references to one's flaws and apparent vileness. One will hope that the enemies will eventually tire, but so long as one is known, one will be tormented.

The search for publicity is, at heart, a quest for a shortcut to friendship. Yet real kindness is never available in a public arena. It is the fruit of a few intimate and reciprocal connections. It cannot be won remotely or one-sidedly. If it is safety one seeks, one must definitively and immediately cease to strive to be known to people one doesn't know and concentrate instead on building up genuine bonds that can survive one's errors and endure for life. Paradoxically and poignantly, it is most often the very anxious who feel a particular longing for the embrace of fame; but it is especially they (given their fragility) who should be warned away from its ultimately always vengeful arms. Being entirely forgotten by the world is no curse or sign of failure; it is the very basis for a contented and safe life in which one swaps the prospect of acolytes and mean-minded detractors for the deeper satisfaction of true friends. The moment anyone becomes famous should always be considered – by those who really care for them – as a time for mourning.

We grow up – inevitably – with a strong attachment to a plan A: that is, an idea of how our lives will go and what we need to do to achieve our particular set of well-defined goals. For example, we'll do four years of law school, then move out west, buy a house and start a family. Or, we'll go to medical school for seven years, then go to another country and train in our speciality of interest and hope to retire by fifty. Or, we'll get married and raise two children with an emphasis on the outdoors and doing good in the world.

But then, for some of us, and at one level all of us, life turns out to have made a few other plans. A sudden injury puts a certain career forever out of reach. A horrible and unexpected bit of office politics blackens our name and forces us out of our professional path. We discover an infidelity or make a small but significant error that changes everything about how crucial others view us.

And so, promptly, we find we have to give up on plan A altogether. The realisation can feel devastating. Sobbing or terrified, we wonder how things could have turned out this way. By what piece of damnation has everything come to this? Who could have predicted that the lively and hopeful little boy or girl we once were would have to end up in such a forlorn and pitiful situation? We alternately weep and rage at the turn of events.

B It is for such moments that we should, even when things appear calm and hopeful, consider one of life's most vital skills: that of developing a plan B.

The first element involves fully acknowledging that we are never cursed for having to make a plan B. Plan As simply do not work out all the time. No one gets through life with all their careful plan As intact. Something unexpected, shocking and abhorrent regularly comes along, not only to us, but to all human beings. We are simply too exposed to accident, too lacking in information, too frail in our capacities, to avoid some serious avalanches and traps.

The second point is to realise that we are, despite moments of confusion, eminently capable of developing very decent plan Bs. The reason why we often don't trust that we can is that children can't so easily – and childhood is where we have all come from and continue to be influenced by in ways it's hard to recognise. When children's plans go wrong, they can't do much in response: they have to stay at the same school, they can't divorce their parents, they can't move to another country or shift job. They're locked in and immobile.

But adults are not at all this way, a glorious fact that we need to keep refreshing in our minds and draw comfort from in anxious moments. We have enormous capacities to act and to adapt. The path ahead may be blocked, but we have notable scope to find other routes through. One door may close, but there truly are many other entrances to try. We do not have only one way through this life, even if – at times – we cling fervently to a picture of how everything should and must be.

We're a profoundly adaptable species. Perhaps we'll have to leave town forever, maybe we'll have to renounce an occupation we spent a decade nurturing, perhaps it will be impossible to remain with someone in whom we had placed great faith.

It can feel desperate – until we rediscover our latent plan B muscle. In reality, there would be a possibility to relocate, to start afresh in another domain, to find someone else, to navigate around the disastrous event. There was no one script for us written at our birth, and nor does there need to be only one going forward.

It helps, in flexing our plan B muscles, to acquaint ourselves with the lives of many others who had to throw away plan As and begin anew: the person who thought they'd be married forever, then suddenly weren't – and coped; the person who was renowned for doing what they did, then had to start over in a dramatically different field – and found a way.

Amidst these stories, we're liable to find a few people who will tell us, very sincerely, that their plan B ended up, eventually, superior to their plan A. They worked harder for it, they had to dig deeper to find it and it carried less vanity and fear within it.

Crucially, we don't need to know right now what our plan Bs might be. We should simply feel confident that we will, if and when we need to, be able to work them out. We don't need to ruminate on them all now or anticipate every frustration that might come our way; we should simply feel confident that, were the universe to command it, we would know how to find a very different path �֍

BUT THEN,
FOR SOME OF US
AND AT ONE LEVEL
ALL OF US,
LIFE TURNS OUT TO
HAVE MADE A FEW
OTHER PLANS.

As is often the case with anxiety, when it comes to relationships, we have a habit of making potentially somewhat frightening situations far worse by downplaying the challenges that are at play.

A good relationship requires that we take a series of unambiguously daunting steps. We are required to give another person the keys to our affection, to our sense of self and to our power to thrive as autonomous beings. We need to make space for them in our bed, in our friendships and in our routines. Along the way, we cede to them the power to upset us with a slightly offhand remark or late response, and the power to devastate us by deciding to call it a day (let alone by holding the hand of a colleague on a business trip). Our anxieties are compounded by any susceptibility to worry created in our minds by our childhood; perhaps these hold experiences of relationships not working out, of parents who argued viciously in front of us, or separated before we could understand why. We may have grown into adults for whom the spectre of the collapse of a relationship is charged with some of the heightened emotion of a bruised and defenceless child. Our societies focus relentlessly on the upsides of the start of love; we would do well to have some sympathy for the terrors.

Unfortunately, when we are scared in love, we have vicious tendencies not to recognise the fact in ourselves – and so to make a hash of explaining our fears to others. Rather than gently laying out that we dread the partner's absence or the occasional insecurity of not knowing quite how they feel about us, we may instead go in for avoidant patterns of behaviour, whereby we claim to be wholly indifferent at precisely the moments when we are most worried and longing for reassurance. Unsure of their love, we insist on our independence – which can provoke them to pull up their drawbridge in turn, initiating a cycle of mutual withdrawal. Or else we may, in the face of our fears of their shifting emotions, try to pin them down procedurally: asking them where they were last night with uncharming suspicion, complaining bitterly if they were a minute late calling us and nagging them to carry out a succession of household chores, which we frame as verdicts on the state of our relationship.

How much better it always is to identify the fear in oneself and share it open-heartedly and guilelessly with our partner. How much more seductive to say 'I'm frightened of losing you' than to behave as though one doesn't care or has turned into a chore-monster. We underestimate the strength we immediately acquire upon admitting that we're presently feeling very weak.

Of course it is terrifying to be in love; that is, to depend on another person we don't control for our happiness. We should never make our anxieties worse by being under any illusion that they shouldn't exist. A contented couple should make regular room, perhaps as often as once a day, for a discussion around the theme of, 'What scares me about depending on you is....' That would be the start of a properly relaxing, and loving, way to live ✳

The anxieties of love may be compounded by even more tortured feelings around sex – another topic about which we are expected, implausibly, not to be scared.

But how foolish to assume that it might not be anything other than very complicated to take one's clothes off in front of someone and attempt to make love with them. Far from being the uninhibited and liberated free spirits that the adverts suggest we all are, many of us bear important legacies of shame around the expression of our sexualities.

Our capacity to express our sexual selves confidently and happily, our ability to say what we want and to ask for it without embarrassment, are enormous psychological achievements. They are also generally only available to those among us who enjoyed highly supportive and emotionally evolved early environments. For us to be sexually untroubled adults requires that, way back, others will have left us feeling acceptable to ourselves: enjoying a sense that our bodies and their functions were natural and fine things, that we were not naughty or sinful for expressing curiosity about ourselves and that it was (for example) more than a good idea to be, at the age of two, properly delighted by the strange and wondrous existence of one's own bottom.

Sexual desire is one of the most personal and vulnerable things that we are ever called upon to express – and it exposes one to potentially momentous degrees of ridicule. As bullies of all kinds have always known, if you want to destroy someone fast, shame them about their sexuality; they'll never have the self-confidence to challenge you again. There are few things more deeply 'us' than our longing for sexual connection; therefore, any feelings of unworthiness – any worries about how nice we are, how deserving we may be or how legitimate it is that we exist – have a sure habit of cropping up in the bedroom and of destroying our ability to be straightforward and unconflicted sexual beings. To generalise crudely, if there is any danger of us feeling bad about ourselves, we're going – by a psychological inevitability – to feel bad about ourselves and sex. What get called sexual problems – impotence, vaginismus, lack of desire, harmful addictions – are, first and foremost, always problems of self-hatred. And one can't, as a rule, both hate oneself and be having a terrific time in bed.

Beginning to repair the problem of sexual shame relies on a basic acceptance that the problem exists and can play havoc with our lives. We need to learn to name and track the matter; despite suggestions to the contrary, a lot of us, women and men, are right now walking the earth intensely ashamed of ourselves sexually – not because what we want sexually is in any objective way 'bad' (that is, disgusting or willingly hurtful to someone else), but because our histories have predisposed us to feel so negatively about our own selfhood.

A central effect of sexual shame is to silence us. We are so embarrassed that we cannot even speak of our embarrassment. It is of huge importance therefore to dare to put our feelings into words and to seek out warm-hearted, broad-minded people with whom we can, in safety, finally admit to our inhibitions – and learn to see ourselves through eyes that are not biased, judgemental or uncaring.

To take a measure of how much shame we are carrying within us, we might along the way ask ourselves a few poignant questions to which we might not have pleasant answers:

> How do you feel about your own body?
> How sorry do you have to feel for a person having sex with you?
> Could someone know you sexually, properly know you, and still like you?

In a caring, mutually supportive environment, our acceptance of our sexuality is one of the most generous and mature acts we're capable of. We – the ashamed ones – deserve to rediscover sex not as a zone of guilt and anxiety but as an intensely fulfilling, innocent and, in the profound sense, 'fun' pastime, something we truly deserve to enjoy in the same way that, despite early intimations to the contrary, we truly deserve to exist ✳

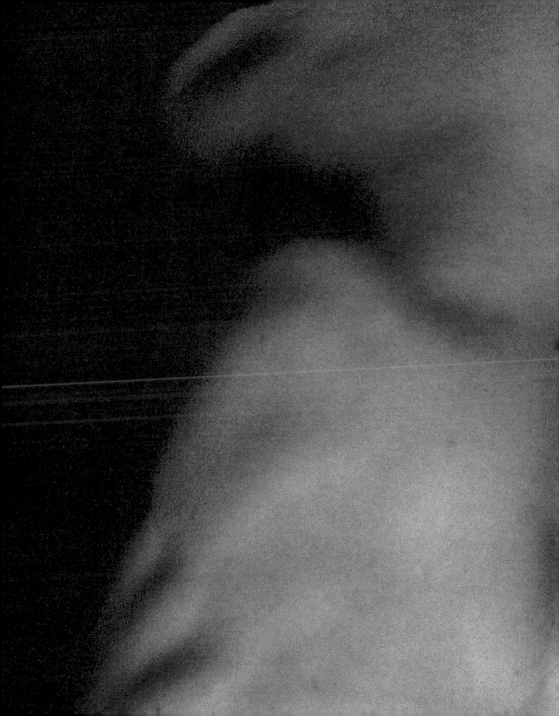

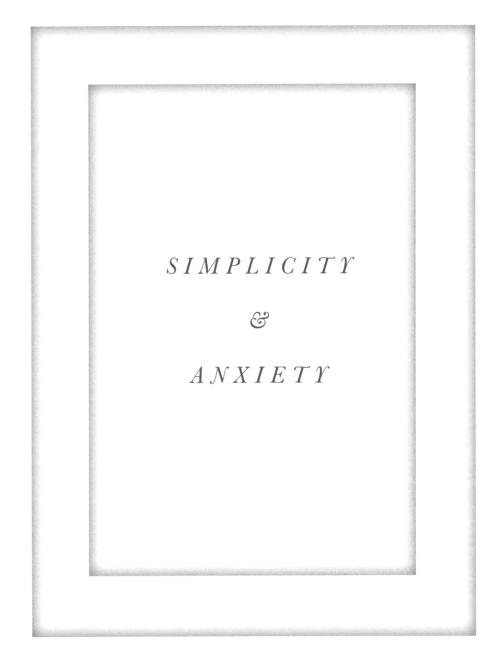

SIMPLICITY

&

ANXIETY

It is well understood by good parents that life should only ever get so exciting for a baby: after friends have come around and brought presents and made animated faces, after there has been some cake and some cuddles, after there have been a lot of bright lights and perhaps some songs too, enough is enough. The baby will start to look stern and then burst into tears and the wise parent knows that nothing is particularly wrong (though the baby may by now be wailing): it is just time for a nap. The brain needs to process, digest and divide up the welter of experiences that have been ingested, and so the curtains are drawn, baby is laid down next to the soft toys and soon it is asleep and calm descends. Everyone knows that life is going to be a lot more manageable again in an hour.

Sadly, we exercise no such caution with ourselves. We schedule a week in which we will see friends every night, in which we'll do twelve meetings (three of them requiring a lot of preparation), where we'll make a quick overnight dash to another country on the Wednesday, where we'll watch three films, read fourteen newspapers, change six pairs of sheets, have five heavy meals after 8pm and drink thirty coffees – and then we lament that our lives are not as calm as they might be and that we are close to mental collapse.

We refuse to take seriously how much of our babyhood is left inside our adult selves – and, therefore, how much care we have to take to keep things simple and very, very calm. What registers as anxiety is typically no freakish phenomenon; it is the mind's logical, enraged plea not to be continuously and exhaustingly overstimulated.

What are some of the things we may need to do to simplify our lives?

_____→

It is theoretically a privilege to have a lot of people to see and things to do. It is also – psychologically speaking – exhausting and ultimately rather dangerous.

The manner of expression is a little dated and brutal, and one might want to quibble over the exact timings, but this point from Friedrich Nietzsche remains acute: 'Today, as always, men fall into two groups: slaves and free men. Whoever does not have two-thirds of his day for himself is a slave, whatever he may be: a statesman, a businessman, an official or a scholar.'

We need to recognise that what is physically possible for us to achieve in a day is not psychologically wise or plausible. It may well be feasible to nip over to a foreign capital or two in a day, and run a company alongside managing a household, but we shouldn't be surprised if such routines ultimately contribute to a breakdown.

Plenty of it, of course: at least seven hours. Or, if we can't manage it, we need at a minimum to recognise fully how much we are deprived, so that we won't aggravate our sorrows by searching for abstruse explanations for them. We don't necessarily have to get divorced, retrain in a completely different profession or move country: we just need to get some more rest.

Media

What we're taking in when we check our phones is perhaps the single greatest contributor to our mental ill-health. For most of history, it was inconceivable that there could ever be such a thing as 'too much news'. Information from political circles or foreign countries was rare, prized and expensive (it was as unlikely that one could gorge oneself on it as one could on chocolate bars). But since the middle of the twentieth century, news has been commodified and, in the process, it has become a major – though still too little known – risk to our mental survival.

Every minute of every day presents us with untold options for filling our minds with the mania, exploits,

*WE DON'T
NECESSARILY
HAVE TO
GET DIVORCED,
RETRAIN IN
A COMPLETELY
DIFFERENT
PROFESSION OR
MOVE COUNTRY:
WE JUST NEED
TO GET SOME
MORE REST.*

disasters, furies, reversals, ambitions, triumphs, insanity and cataclysms of strangers around our benighted planet. Always, news organisations speak of our need to know – and our need to know right now. But what they have left out is our equally great, and often even greater, need not to know: because we cannot change anything, because the stories are too violent, dispiriting and sad, because our minds are fragile, because we have responsibilities closer to home, because we need to lead our own lives rather than be torn apart by stories of the lives of others who are ultimately as remote from and irrelevant to us as the inhabitants of the Egyptian court of King Sneferu in late 2613 B.C.

Nutrition

It is maddening to be told this constantly and in such specific and ever-changing detail, but we do – in brief – have to eat less, and simpler things too. The exact details of an anxious person's diet are perhaps for others to argue about, but suffice to say that it should probably involve some hazelnuts, slices of apple, olives, apricots and coarse bread. The body needs long periods unoccupied with any sort of physical digestion to stand a

chance of tackling the endless peculiar fruits of its turbulent mind.

Thinking

Insomnia and anxiety are the mind's revenge for all the thoughts we refuse to have consciously in the day. In order to be able to find rest, we need to carve off chunks of time where we have nothing to do other than lie in bed with a pad and paper in order to think. We need to consider three topics in particular:

> What is making me anxious?
> Who has caused me pain and how?
> What is exciting me?

We need to sift through the chaotic contents of our minds. Every hour of living requires at least ten minutes of sifting. We need to orient ourselves in the ongoing story of our lives by (as it were) writing its next few paragraphs.

We should do some anticipatory thinking as well. On another sheet of paper, we should write, 'What is coming up'. With some of the same patience as a parent taking a child through what it will need to do at school the next day (as has already been established, we need to be better parents to ourselves), we should anticipate the challenges ahead: what time we'll need to order the taxi, how we'll need to schedule some calls, what it might feel like to have a grim conversation with a colleague. Experiences lose at least half of their power to unnerve us when we have gone through them in our minds the day before. We need to recover a sense of the seriousness and dignity of making lists.

Expectations

Of course, it might be pleasant to be extraordinary, famous and world-beating, but maybe it will be an even greater achievement to stay sane and kind. We might opt not to conquer the world in favour of living a longer and more serene life. We are not backing away from a challenge; we're shifting our sense of what the real challenge might be – and, more importantly, where the real rewards may lie. A quiet life isn't necessarily one of resignation or flight; it may constitute a supremely wise recognition that the truly satisfying things are available away from the spotlight and the big cities, on modest salaries and as far as possible from the manic, sleepless competition to 'win' the professional status race.

Beauty

It would be deeply helpful if we could be calm whatever the view was like or however our room was decorated. But we are, as we're establishing, far more sensitive than that. Just as it may help a baby if its room is a gentle shade of lilac, so too it will help our inner state immeasurably if there are very few objects in our visual field and if the ones that are there are in visual harmony (ideally with some bilateral symmetry and repetition of forms). Outer mess inflames any tendency to inner confusion.

The visual world can't magically translate itself into a mood, but it can certainly foster and invite one. We need to take every step we can to make a home in the sort of environment that promises at a visual level the calm we crave at a psychological one.

As we're discovering, excitement is fun for a time; but it also kills. Simplicity is true wisdom.

We need more naps and more white rooms ❊

Magnus von Wright and Wilhelm von Wright, Bird illustration from
Svenska Foglar (Swedish Birds), 1929

The temptation, when we are worried, is to direct our determined intelligence to trying fully to anticipate whatever may be coming for us down the line. We try to strip the unknown of its surprises; we seek, quite understandably, to do nothing less than control the future.

This is far from foolish; there is lots to be learnt from arduous anticipation and rational planning. But, after we have weighed up all possible prognoses and taken every step these might reasonably demand, there is also a moment to confront an apparently maddening, but in reality – if we can approach it from the right angle – highly releasing, thought: we can't ever tell exactly what will happen to us and nor should we try. A great part of our lives lies in the hands of the unknown, in the current of time, in the province of fate. Our minds, however impressive, cannot peer into the future and wrestle it of every last ambiguity. We are subject to too many variables. Our mental telescopes only permit us to see so far. We must learn to sleep on the pillow of doubt.

To help us foster the right kind of scepticism, we should equip ourselves with an attitude of benevolent trust in the face of our ignorance. One of its clearest expressions in Western culture can be found in the sixth chapter of the Gospel of St Matthew, where Jesus – in his Sermon on the Mount – recommends that we quell our anxieties as to where precisely our next meal will come from by looking at the behaviour of birds:

> 'Behold the fowls of the air: for they sow not, neither
> do they reap, nor gather into barns; yet your heavenly
> Father feedeth them. Are ye not much better than they?'

We don't need to believe in a divine creator, or indeed relinquish every sensible attempt to forward plan, to see the wisdom of the point. For all the astonishing powers of our minds, there is a critical role for knowing how to switch them off in the face of uncertainty. We should not torture ourselves with manic, insistent rumination on what cannot yet be known or commanded.

Unknown Flemish painter, *Landscape with Cows*, circa 1870

Beneath Christianity, we sense the origins of such trust: in our childhood experience of fathers and mothers who imbued us with a confidence to navigate the uncharted future, who had faith that we would find a little place to eat along the way, even if we didn't know its name right now. It is never too late to fill in for the absence of such lessons. We can replace God with terms like nature, fate or the universe. We can't tell exactly what will have happened by next year, what the outcome of the test is going to be, who we will love, how our career will pan out or when we will die. But what we can trust is that, whatever unfolds, we will – broadly – be fine. Even death is endurable.

Amongst Nietzsche's more unusual loves were cows, whom he considered the most philosophical of all the animals. In a section of *Thus Spake Zarathustra*, he wrote: 'Unless we change (or be converted) and become as cows, we shall not enter the kingdom of heaven.' What lent the cows their particular wisdom in Nietzsche's eyes was their advanced capacity not to worry overly about their own futures; they knew how to sit quietly in a field, occasionally swatting away a determined fly, chewing strands of meadow grass and taking each minute as it comes. For all their mental limitations, they had achieved something the human mind is extremely bad at: resigning itself to the limits of what can plausibly be known and leaving the rest aside. The real symbols of a thinking life should not, in this vein, be a volume of Montaigne or Plato, but a well-positioned and suitably reverential image of a cow.

We hear no end of reminders as to the benefits of intellectual work. We need, along the way, to rediscover the art of knowing when to cease trying to think ✳

There is, in our quest to master anxiety, a need to face down our fears, to refuse to be cowed and tortured by them – a defiant will not to be defeated by our malignant worries. There may well be an alarm ringing in our head, warning us against new plans and occasions, but we may choose not to listen to it. It can ring all it likes; we may by now have had enough of being bullied by it.

Part of this facing down of anxiety involves a rather surprising move: thinking about the very worst in a great deal of detail – in order to realise that we could, if need be, cope with it. Even if all our circumstances were thrown into reverse, we could survive. Anxiety feeds off our impression of our vulnerability: our sense that we need perfect health, a great reputation, an unblemished record, a lot of money, happiness and love in order to exist. But we can go in the opposite direction and ask ourselves with new rigour what it would be OK not to have, a question that isn't popular with merchandisers but is exceptionally useful for us to turn over, especially in bed at night. We know it could always be better, but in what ways could it be worse, and still – despite everything – bearable?

Rather than shunning thoughts of disasters, we should drain them of their power to scare us by being entirely at home with them. We should think through every bad scenario until we're almost bored and thereby closer to indifference. Anxieties thrive by not being thought about, by festering in the dank corners of the mind; they demand that we pay them attention but hate us to think through them properly. So, we need to introduce them to the bright sunshine of focused thought, give ourselves a pad of paper, plenty of time to reflect and encouragement to ask ourselves: So what would it be if like if X or Y happened...?

And we will tend to find that even if X or Y did come to pass, it would be survivable. The worst, the very worst that can happen is that we die, an eventuality that has happened to a lot of people already and – it appears – they coped well enough.

These kinds of thoughts belong to Stoicism, a philosophy it is hard not to fall back on when dealing with anxiety. Arguably the greatest, and certainly the most prolific, Stoic philosopher was the Roman author and statesman Seneca, who was born in 4 B.C. in Spain and died in 65 A.D. in Rome.

A lot of Seneca's thought is known to us from the letters he wrote to his friends, giving them counsel at times of trouble. Seneca had a friend called Lucilius, a civil servant working in Sicily. One day Lucilius learnt of a lawsuit against him that threatened to end his career and disgrace his good name. He wrote to Seneca in a panic.

'You may expect that I will advise you to picture a happy outcome, and to rest in the allurements of hope,' replied the philosopher, but 'I am going to conduct you to peace of mind through another route' – which culminated in the advice: 'If you wish to put off all worry, assume that what you fear *may* happen is certainly *going* to happen'.

This is an essential Stoic tenet. We must always try to picture the worst that could happen – and then remind ourselves that the worst is survivable. The goal is not to imagine that bad things don't unfold; it is to see that we are far more capable of enduring them than we currently think.

To calm Lucilius down, Seneca advised him to make himself entirely at home with the idea of humiliation, poverty and ongoing unemployment – but to learn to see that these were, from the right perspective, not the end of everything. 'If you lose this case, can anything more severe happen to you than being sent into exile or led to prison?' asked the philosopher, who had himself survived bankruptcy and eight years of exile in Corsica. 'Hope for that which is utterly just, and prepare yourself for that which is utterly unjust.'

Seneca gave Lucilius a meditation to mull over in the luxury of his home that he was now in danger of losing:

'I may become a poor man; I shall then be one among many. I may be exiled; I shall then regard myself as born in the place to which I shall be sent. They may put me in chains. What then? Am I free from bonds now? Behold this clogging burden of a body, to which nature has fettered me!'

Seneca tells us that we must grow familiar with, and hold before us at all times, not just the sort of events we like to plan for, that are recorded in living memory or are common in our age group and class, but the entire range of possibilities – a longer and inevitably far less agreeable list that finds space for cataclysmic fires, sackings and deaths.

'Nothing ought to be unexpected by us. Our minds should be sent forward in advance to meet all problems, and we should consider, not what is wont to happen, but what can happen. Let us place before our eyes in its entirety the nature of man's lot... not the kind of evil that often happens, but the very greatest evil that can possibly happen. We must reflect upon fortune fully and completely.'

At one point, a friend of Seneca's lost a son, and the consoling thoughts ran in a similar direction. Marcia, a lady of a senatorial family, was devastated by the death of her son Metilius, who was not yet twenty-five. She fell into a period of mourning that seemed to have no end. Three years after his death, her sorrow had not abated; indeed, it was growing stronger every day.

So, Seneca sent her an essay in which he expressed the hope that, given the length of time that had elapsed since Metilius's death, she would forgive him for going beyond the usual condolences to deliver something darker, but perhaps more effective.

To lose a son was surely the greatest grief that could befall a mother, but, given the vulnerability of the human frame, Metilius's early death had its place in a merciless natural order, which daily offered examples of its handiwork.

He wrote: 'We never anticipate evils before they actually arrive, but, imagining that we ourselves are exempt and are travelling a less exposed path, we refuse to be taught by the mishaps of others that such are the lot of all. So many funerals pass our doors, yet we never dwell on death. So many deaths are untimely, yet we make plans for our own infants: how they will don the toga, serve in the army and succeed to their father's property.'

They might end up doing such things, but how mad to love them without remembering that no one had offered us a guarantee they would grow to maturity, let alone make it to dinner time.

'No promise has been given you for this night – no, I have suggested too long a respite – no promise has been given even for this hour.'

If Metilius's death had been unexpected for Marcia, it was only on the basis of a wishful assessment of probabilities.

'You say: "I did not think it would happen." Do you think there is anything that will not happen, when you know that it is possible to happen, when you see that it has already happened to many?'

Seneca imagined meeting Marcia before her birth and inviting her on a tour of the troubled earth so that she could weigh up the terms of life, then choose whether or not to accept them. On the one hand, Marcia would see a planet of awe-inspiring beauty; on the other, a place of constant, unspeakable horror. Would Marcia choose to step into such a world? Her existence suggested her answer. In which case, would she not now have to bow to the real terms of earthly life?

Importantly, the Stoics and Seneca thought that if things were really unendurable, we had no obligation to continue forever:

'The wise man will live as long as he ought, not as long as he can.... He always reflects concerning the quality, and not the quantity, of his life. As soon as there are numerous events in his life that give him trouble and disturb his peace of mind, he sets himself free. And this privilege is his, not only when the crisis is upon him, but as soon as Fortune seems to be maltreating him; then he looks about carefully and sees whether he ought, or ought not, to end his life on that account.

'He holds that it makes no difference to him whether his taking off be natural or self-inflicted, whether it comes later or earlier. He does not regard it with fear, as if it were a great loss; for no man can lose very much when but a driblet remains. It is not a question of dying earlier or later, but of dying well or ill. And dying well means escape from the danger of living ill.'

Seneca was not advocating random or thoughtless exits; he was attempting to give us more courage in the face of anxiety by reminding us that it is always within our remit, when we have genuinely tried everything and rationally had enough, to choose a noble path out of our troubles.

He was seeking to strip willed death of its associations with pathology and to render it instead an option that the wise always know is there as a backstop.

When we are furious, paranoid, depleted or sad, the philosophy of Stoicism is on hand – as it has been for 2,000 years – to nurse us with its hugely fortifying, distinctive and unusual wisdom and friendship ✳

Manuel Domínguez Sánchez, *The Death of Seneca*, 1871

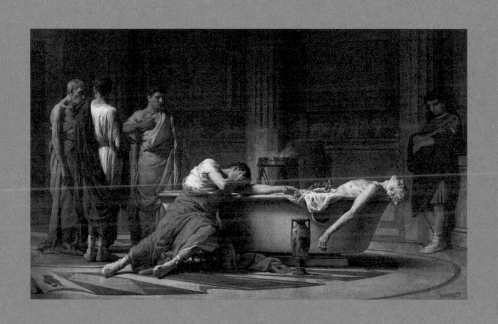

What most of us long for above all else is 'security', the sense that we are – at last – safe on the earth. We pin our hopes for security on a shifting array of targets: a happy relationship, a house, children, a good profession, public respect, a certain sum of money.... When these are ours, we fervently believe we will finally be at peace. We may mock the term 'happily ever after', synonymous as it is with naive children's literature, but in practice we do, indeed, tend to live as if we could one day, somewhere over the horizon, reach a place of rest, satisfaction and safety.

It's therefore worth trying to understand why happiness 'ever after' should be congenitally so impossible. It isn't that we can't ever have a good relationship, a house or a pension. We may well have all this – and more. It's simply that these won't be able to deliver what we hope for from them. We will still worry in the arms of a kind and interesting partner, we will still fret in a well-appointed kitchen, our terrors won't cease whatever income we have. It sounds implausible – especially when these goods are still far out of our grasp – but we should trust this fundamental truth in order to make an honest peace with the forbidding facts of the human condition.

We can never properly be secure, because so long as we are alive, we will be alert to danger and, in some way, at risk. The only people with full security are the dead; the only people who can be truly at peace are under the ground. Cemeteries are the only definitively calm places around.

There is a certain nobility in coming to accept this fact – and the unending nature of worry in our lives. We should both recognise the intensity of our desire for a happy endpoint and at the same time acknowledge the inbuilt reasons why it cannot be ours.

We should give up on the Arrival Fallacy, the conviction that there might be such a thing as a destination, in the sense of a stable position beyond which we will no longer suffer, crave and dread.

The feeling that there must be such a point of arrival begins in childhood, with a longing for certain toys; then the destination shifts, perhaps to love, or career. Other popular destinations include children and family, fame, retirement or (even) 'after the novel is published'.

It isn't that these places don't exist. It's just that they aren't places that we can pull up at, settle in, feel adequately sheltered by and never want to leave again. None of these zones will afford us a sense that we have properly arrived. We will soon enough discover threats and restlessness anew.

One response is to imagine that we may be craving the wrong things, that we should look elsewhere, perhaps to something more esoteric or high-minded: philosophy or beauty, community or art.

But that is just as illusory. It doesn't matter what goals we have: they will never be enough. Life is a process of replacing one anxiety and one desire with another. No goal spares us renewed goal seeking. The only stable element in our lives is craving; the only destination is the journey.

What are the implications of fully accepting the Arrival Fallacy? We may still have ambitions, but we'll have a certain ironic detachment about what is likely to happen when we fulfil them. We'll know the itch will start up again soon enough. Knowing the Arrival Fallacy, we'll be subject to illusion, but at least aware of the fact. When we watch others striving, we may experience slightly less envy. It may look as if certain others have reached 'there'. But we know they are still longing and worrying in the mansions of the rich and the suites of CEOs.

We should naturally try to give the journey more attention: we should look out of the window and appreciate the view whenever we can. But we should also understand why this can only ever be a partial solution. Our longing is too powerful a force. The greatest wisdom we're capable of is to know why true wisdom won't be fully possible – and instead pride ourselves on having at least a slight oversight on our madness.

We can accept the ceaselessness of certain anxieties and rather than aim for a calm, yogic state, serenely accept that we will never be definitely calm. Our goal should not be to banish anxiety but to learn to manage, live well around and – when we can – heartily laugh at, our anxious state ✳

The majority of our lives requires us to be heavily invested in our own ego, its pleasures, sufferings and ambitions. But we are also capable, at rare moments, of accessing a mood of detachment in which what exactly happens to us, who we are and what we are capable of cease to be of such primary and tortuous concern – and we are able to look out at the world as if we were not so condemned to be so tightly connected to ourselves.

In such moods of detachment, which can take place particularly at night, often in the vastness of nature, practical concerns are, for a time, kept wholly at bay and we accede to an unnerving yet thrillingly oblique perspective on existence. We might be driving down a deserted motorway or looking down at the earth from a plane tracing its way across Greenland. It might be high summer or a deep winter evening. The essential element is that we are able to look 'beyond the ego'. Helped along by the sound of flowing water or the call of a distant owl, the habitual struggle ceases, we are freed from our customary egoistic vigilance and we can do a properly extraordinary thing: look at life as if we were not us, as if we were a roaming eye that could inhabit the perspective of anyone or anything else, a foreigner or a child, a crab on a seashore or a cloud on the hazy horizon. In our detached state, the 'I', the vessel that we are usually supremely and exhaustively loyal to, ceases to be our primary responsibility. We can take our leave and become a roaming, vagabond, promiscuous thing, a visitor of other mentalities and modalities, as concerned with all that is not us as we are normally obsessed by what is.

As a result, a range of emotions that we would typically feel only in relation to us can be experienced around other elements too. We might feel the pain of someone we hardly know, or be gratified by the success of a stranger. We could take pride in a beauty or intelligence to which we were wholly unconnected. We can be imaginative participants in the entire cosmic drama.

There might, in all this, be a particular emphasis on love. That could sound odd, because we're used to thinking of love in a very particular context, that of the circumscribed affection that one person might have for a very accomplished and desirable other. But understood properly, love involves a care and concern for anything at all. We might find ourselves loving – that is, appreciating and delighting in, understanding and sympathising with – a family of dung beetles or a moss-covered tundra, someone else's child or the birth of a faraway star. An intensity of enthusiasm that we usually restrict to only one other nearby ego can be distributed more erratically and generously across the entire universe and all its life forms.

No longer so closely wedded to ourselves, we cease to worry overly about what might happen to our puny and vulnerable selves in the always uncertain future. We may be readier to give up on some of our jealously guarded and pedantically held goals. We may never get to quite where we want to go, but we are more prepared to bob on the eddies of life, content to let events buffet us as they may. We make our peace with the laws of entropy. We may never be properly loved or appropriately appreciated. We'll die before everything has been achieved – and that will be OK.

And yet, at the same time, a particular gaiety might descend on us, for a huge amount of our energy is normally directed towards nursing our ego's wounds and coping with what we deep down suspect is the utter indifference of others. But that no longer seems like a spectre we have to ward off and we can start to raise our eyes and notice life in a way we never otherwise do. Our invisibility and meaninglessness is a given we now joyfully accept, rather than angrily or fearfully rage against. We don't quake in fear that we might not be a somebody; we embrace the full knowledge of our eternal nullity – and delight that, right now, the blossom looks truly enchanting in the field opposite.

We cannot persist at a detached plane at all times; there will inevitably be bills to be paid and children to be picked up. But the claims of the ordinary world do not invalidate or mock our occasional access to a more elevated and disinterested zone, in which the burden of being us is momentarily lifted and, with the usual thrum of anxiety stilled, we can pay due heed to what is always there, waiting for us to be in a state to notice: the wonder and beauty of existence ✳

Given how much we all long to be happy, we might presume that accepting the possibility of happiness in our lives would be an uncomplicated, serene and automatic process. But for many of us, however theoretically attached we might be to the notion of being happy, the possibility of actually being so is liable to trigger deep ambivalence and fear. We would – it appears – often prefer to be worried and sad rather than attempt to take on the risks surreptitiously connected in our minds with positive moods. We may – however paradoxical it sounds – be nothing less than afraid to be happy.

As ever, our fear has a history that begins in childhood, where one of the following is likely to have occurred. Someone we deeply loved, and perhaps admired too, was unhappy. Their sorrow moved us profoundly and led us to identify with them so that our caution around contentment continues to function as a secret tribute to them. To be happy would, in a way that would pain us profoundly, mean being disloyal. However much they might on the surface have encouraged us to venture out and seize opportunities for joy, an important part of us wishes to stay with them under the canopy of grief. So without knowing we're doing this, we ensure that we will always have a modest career because they never had educational possibilities, or we turn down sexual opportunities because they were sexually neglected. Alternatively, someone we were close to might have been jealous of us and led us to want to downplay our achievements and hide our contentment – in order to feel safe from their envy and rage. Or perhaps we were badly let down by someone in whom we had once placed a lot of hope – and now it feels more appropriate to anticipate a blow rather than be surprised by one. We learnt to associate gloom with safety and joy with risk. More generally, we may have lacked any plausible role models for happiness. We may have grown up in an environment where being anxious and panicky was the default state, where it seemed natural to picture the plane crashing, the police showing up, the business collapsing and the mole turning malignant. We may be intellectually aware that there could be other ways to interpret the future, but equanimity doesn't feel like what our tribe does. To this resistance, we might have added a layer of intellectual superiority. Deep in our hearts, we might suspect that happiness is for the little people, and that the leading symptom of understanding the world intelligently must be sadness.

All such positions contribute to a psyche where the onset of happiness is a cause for grave and glaring alarm. When we are finally on holiday, in love, surrounded by friends or free of financial pressure, we panic. Our senses have been jammed for so long in fear mode they are filled with dread when the alarm stops wailing.

To return to a more balanced state, we're liable systematically to sabotage the conditions of contentment. We start working on holiday and soon uncover a cause for concern at the office; within hours, we may be protesting that we need to return home. Or else we do our utmost to convince a new lover that we're not worth it, by seldom calling them or (if they really don't get the message) having an affair. It feels so much more normal to be abandoned.

In order to acclimatise ourselves to joy, we need to return to the past and unpick how we learnt to use anxiety as a defensive strategy to protect us against other threats we were too young and too easily overwhelmed to answer.

The manic worrier worries, as it were, about 'everything' because they are unable to be appropriately concerned with, and in mourning for, one or two big things from long ago. The anxiety that belonged to one particular distant time and place has been redistributed and subdivided across hundreds of ever shifting topics in the present (from workplace to reputation, money to household tasks), because its true source and origins remain unknown to the sufferer.

We are using the flotsam and jetsam of everyday worries as a proxy for an unmasterable trauma: shame; humiliation; a sense that we don't matter to our caregivers; neglect or abuse. We should not sarcastically point out to worriers that they need 'something else to worry about', we should realise that something terrifying that they have buried deep in their unconscious is lending a continuous sense of dread to their fragile present.

We manic worriers need not sarcasm but supportive and intelligent company to give us the love we need to dare to look back at the past – and the insight with which to try to do so. Our dread is a symptom of an ancient sorrow, a sign that we keep not finding anything in the outer world that answers to the horror of the inner one.

Needless to say, it isn't the case that there is never anything to worry about in the present, just that there is a lot less than the manic worrier tends to believe. Furthermore, what there is to worry about can be coped with with far more resilience than the manic worrier can imagine, for they are operating with what is essentially a child's sense of their own powers and capacity for survival. Manic worriers should gradually come to exchange their feelings of dread for the future for a patient understanding and mourning for an unfairly traumatic and as yet insufficiently explored past.

There is nothing greedy or stupid about happiness. The ability to take appropriate satisfaction from the good times is a profound psychological achievement: it is a mark of deep seriousness to be able to giggle, have a pillow fight with a child, delight in a fig, sunbathe, sometimes knock off work early to have an ice cream and appreciate a daffodil. Sorrow is obvious; there is always a richness of reasons to despair. Fear is safe as well; if we are waiting for the enemy with sword in hand, we may gain a vital few seconds were the blow to come. But the truly courageous and heroically defiant move (given our background) would be to dare to put down our weapon, lessen our preparations for catastrophe, resist the terrors ingrained in us over decades and once in a while believe that, astonishingly, for a time, there might truly be nothing to worry about ❊

AN IDEAL

LIFE FOR

THE

ANXIOUS

However much we often claim that we would like not to be so anxious, we seldom systematically undertake truly concerted efforts not to be. Our moves, in so far as we make them, tend to be modest and intermittent: a book here or there, the odd candle, a trip to the countryside, a New Year's vow to do less and think more. Yet we hold back from fundamentally rearranging our activities in the name of a more serene life. We let our ambitions for calm take a backseat to other, more standard and noisy priorities: making money, raising a family, gaining status.

It might therefore be revealing, as a thought experiment, to try to imagine what a life might look like in its details if one actually did raise calm to our overwhelming priority; if – from dawn until bedtime – all our practical and psychological goals had an untroubled state of mind as their target. Given all that we have learnt about anxiety – its origins, triggers and salves – what might some of the features of a pervasively calm life look like?

Living together

For a start, we would probably seek to live together, communally, away from the loneliness of a single life or the fractiousness of a nuclear family unit, among a group of people similarly committed to containing anxiety – but also similarly sensitive to losing their grip on calm. The ideal community would be marked by kindness, gentleness and great sympathy for the troubles of being human. Among such people, there would be no pressure to impress or to deny one's sorrows and worries. Everyone would be open to the idea that they were a little 'broken' – while simultaneously profoundly committed to the business of repair and generosity.

Christian monks understood early on that living as part of a community governed by an ideal would require a particular kind of architectural setting and location. The monasteries that sprang up around Europe in the Dark Ages enforced their spiritual commitments with very specific architectural features: massive stone walls, bare but noble furnishings, inner courtyards, communal dining tables, kitchen gardens and simple – though often elegant – cells equipped with a bed, a desk and a narrow view out onto open country. The monasteries were typically situated far from cities, so that their members could concentrate on their studies and thoughts, while regularly drawing inspiration from the sublimity of nature.

There are obvious differences between a life devoted to God and one devoted to calm, but we can imagine being no less purposeful in the design of a community for serenity. An ideal such community might, for example, be situated in one of the more remote Canary Islands (El Hierro or La Gomera), so that members could enjoy a constantly mild, light and agreeable climate, a fresh, light vegetable-based diet, groves of almond, lemon and mango trees and, at night, reminders of humanity's redemptively small place in the wider scheme derived from the exceptionally clear, pollution-free views onto the cosmos above.

There would, we can imagine, be dispersed bedrooms around the property, a large dining room, a library, space for meetings – and colonnades around which to walk and share pieces of one's inner life.

Gatherings

Every day in this ideal architectural setting, one would gather in a group and share whatever was in danger of engulfing or troubling one: there might be a discussion on shame or childhood neglect, anger or passivity. The purpose of such group discussions would be to foster a mood of communal introspection and strengthen every individual's commitment to understanding and soothing themselves. Any feeling that one was an outcast would regularly be diminished by the spirit of honest confession and candid interaction.

*Concept drawings, a School of Life
Community for Serenity*

Psychotherapy

As a substitute for the religious instruction of monasteries, there would – in the Community for the Anxious – be a full complement of the best psychotherapists. Once a day, one would be able to sit with someone expertly trained to listen to, and make sense of, the confusions of one's mind. To the sound of a trickling fountain outside, the therapist would tease out one's more reticent and defensive aspects, help one feel compassionate towards one's younger self, untangle dreams and fears – and teach one how to trust anew and communicate maturely with other people.

Time for reflection

A lot of the time, in the Community for the Anxious, one would be free of commitments and able to sit on one's own, downloading the contents of one's mind, while sitting in an elegantly appointed but very simple room (perhaps with a glimpse of a fig tree outside). One would work through outstanding anxieties, run through historic hurts and analyse where one's life might go next.

> ### 'I'VE BEEN SO BUSY' WOULD BE ONE OF THE MOST SHOCKING THINGS ONE COULD SAY TO OTHERS.

Routines

Life in the Community would, in the best sense, be very boring. There would be no newspapers or screens. What was happening beyond the island would be a matter of deep indifference (except in so far as it had urgent relevance). Every day would be much like any other. One wouldn't be trying to do anything very complicated. An achievement might be to help to rake the courtyard or rearrange some books in the library. The therapeutic value of cooking, housekeeping and gardening would be fully recognised – and rather than being seen as demeaning tasks, these would be framed as calming and essential. 'I've been so busy' would be one of the most shocking things one could say to others. All the glamour would centre around being able to reveal that one had done not very much at all other than think, talk and rest.

No status race

Because one would be among sincere friends, there would be no attempts to jockey for position or assert one's superiority. Being famous or rich would lose any meaning because the only currencies in operation would be those of sincerity and kindness.

Good habits

The Community would recognise that the great enemy of a good life is that we have the wrong habits. It isn't that we don't know in theory what would help us; we simply have no mechanism for instilling the right behaviours in practice. So the Community would impose a deliberately rather bossy set of routines, not in order to trap us, but in order to liberate us to be the calm people we anyway long to be. The diary for the day might look like this:

6.30–7 a.m.	Wake up, wash and dress
7–7.30 a.m.	Exercise
7.30–8.30 a.m.	Communal breakfast
8.30–10 a.m.	Time alone in room to think and reflect
10–11 a.m.	Psychotherapy
11 a.m.–1 p.m.	Housework
1–2 p.m.	Communal lunch
2–3 p.m.	Siesta
3–4 p.m.	A walk with a friend
4–6 p.m.	Friendship groups
6–7 p.m.	Reading, learning (especially study of Stoicism and psychotherapy)
7–8 p.m.	Dinner
8–11 p.m.	Study of the stars
11 p.m.	Sleep

It would – of course – be very hard for us to live like this, but this deliberately somewhat dramatic proposal at least gives us a sense of what we might need to do if we are sincere in our aspirations to lead calmer lives. Given that an unagitated state truly is one of the most fulfilling and rewarding of modalities, we might dare to make a few major moves. We are anxious not only out of our innate biological dispositions (though these don't help), but chiefly because we don't structure our lives properly so as to counteract our panicky natures. And given that we rarely obtain what we don't plan for, we are about as worried as we can be expected to be – in the conditions we have built for ourselves.

For too much of our own lives, and for too long in the course of human history, we have left calm to chance. We owe it to ourselves to start more consciously to build the calm lives we so deeply crave and could so richly benefit from ✳

Published in 2020 by The School of Life
First published in the USA in 2020
70 Marchmont Street, London, WC1N 1AB

Copyright © The School of Life 2020

Printed in Latvia by Livonia
Designed and typeset by Marcia Mihotich

A proportion of this book has appeared online at
www.theschooloflife.com/thebookoflife

The School of Life is a resource for helping us
understand ourselves, for improving our relationships,
our careers and our social lives – as well as for helping
us find calm and get more out of our leisure hours.
We do this through creating films, workshops, books
and gifts.

www.theschooloflife.com

ISBN 978-1-912891-21-4

10 9 8 7 6 5 4 3

Picture credits:

10   Rock Balance. Kane / Flickr
15   Tension. Pixel Addict / Flickr
16   The colour of the sky towards evening. Gilberto
     Taccari / Flickr
26   Pixabay / Pixels
36   Christina Morillo / Pixels
40   Boethius, Consolation. Austrian National Library
     /Picryl
41   Miniature of Philosophy from *Le Livre de Boece
     de Consolacion (Consolation of Philosophy)*,
     15th century. The British Library, London / Picryl
42   French Miniaturist (15th century). *Fortune and
     Her Wheel*: Illustration from Vol. 1 of
     Boccaccio's *De Casibus Virorum Illustrium (On
     the Fates of Famous Men)*, 1467, Glasgow,
     Glasgow University Library. © Bridgeman Art
     Library
43   Fortuna, Roman reworking from a Greek
     original, circa 4th century BC. Sailko /
     Wikimedia Commons
46   Man with mobile phone. Robert Scarth / Flickr
50   Free Nature Stock / Pixels
53   Pietro Jeng / Pixels
58   New Year's Eve rockets illuminate the New Year's
     sky over Bloemendaal in the Netherlands. Marco
     Verch / Flickr
63   Cracks. Crispin Semmens / Flickr
66   Thaís Silva / Pexels
76   Magnus von Wright and Wilhelm von Wright,
     Bird illustration from *Svenska Foglar (Swedish
     Birds)*, digitally enhanced from the 1929 folio
     version of Svenska Foglar. Rawpixel / Wikimedia
     Commons
78   Unknown Flemish painter, *Landscape with
     Cows*, circa 1870. Oil on oak panel, 39 cm x 53 cm.
     Private collection
80   Peeling White Paint on Morter.
     José Ramón Polo López / Flickr
82   Volcano. Din Muhammad Sumon / Flickr
87   Manuel Domínguez Sánchez, *The Death of
     Seneca*, 1871. Oil on Canvas, 270 cm x 450 cm.
     Museo del Prado, Madrid
88 (t) Nick Knezic / Pexels
88 (b) Oleg Magni / Pexels
91   John Donges / Flickr
100 Balloons. LuxFactory / Flickr
103-4 Tamsin Hanke / Sash Scott (THISS)
     http://www.thiss.works

The School of Life is a global organisation helping people lead more fulfilled lives. It is a resource for helping us understand ourselves, for improving our relationships, our careers and our social lives – as well as for helping us find calm and get more out of our leisure hours. We do this through films, workshops, books, gifts and community. You can find us online, in stores and in welcoming spaces around the globe.